Originally published by the authors in 1973 as two pamphlets, this contribution to a theory of sexuality and sexual politics is out of print in its original form. It is here republished as a book jointly by Red Collective and Publications Distribution Cooperative.

SARAH

The Politics of Sexuality in Capitalism

Red Collective

Published jointly by Red Collective and Publications Distribution Cooperative
Typeset by Bread 'n Roses, 30 Camden Road, London NW1
Design and artwork by M, 232 Mare Street, London E8
Printed by Blackrose Press, 30 Clerkenwell Close, London EC1

Hardback ISBN 0 906423 01 5
Paperback ISBN 0 906423 00 7

Trade distribution by PDC, 27 Clerkenwell Close, London EC1 01-251 4976

Typeset in 10 on 12 IBM Press Roman medium

CONTENTS

PAMPHLET ONE

THE CONTEXT OF SEXUAL POLITICS

A difficulty about sexual politics is that you cannot think about feelings when you are within them, and you can't help being within them when you are within particular structures of relationships. We need to work out a practice within which to make concrete our understanding of how the family sustains capitalism. For a concrete sexual politics we need to know how the forms of feeling which are the basis of sexual relations inside and outside the family are related to the family's functions. These are aspects of the family, connected with, but not reducible to, the sexual power structure of male domination which has received most study and challenge from the women's movement up till now.

People have feelings and are sexual within particular structures of relationships: the monogamous couple is a structure which combines sex and love; there are diverse forms of the family that arise as the family in its old patriarchal form disintegrates and fails to confine love and sex; there is an extreme form of casual sexual relationship which disjoins sex from emotional, and all other, forms of bonds. These structures of relationships are within a system of social relations which determines the internal quality of the emotional and sexual.

As an example, the social separation of the contexts of work and the family means that the people you love are not the people with whom you necessarily have working relationships. This is the case both for men and women, and it means that the kinds of feelings are different from a society where a man and a woman work alongside each other (as in pre-capitalist, peasant societies) and are related to each other by another visible bond which is not purely sexual and personal. In our society, couples do depend on each other's labour, but it is not in a concrete context of working together. We only feel we love each other because we love each other: the relationship is its own raison d'etre. Emotional relationships, friendship as well as love, are abstracted out of other activities. And since women's work has been at home, her whole existence has been confined to one side of this separation, and so she is placed to experience love differently from the man. So, while a man and a woman in a couple love each other, the feelings and the dynamics of this relationship are not the same for each of them.

The system of social relations within which these feelings occur is not at all transparent. This is why it is enormously difficult to think about sexuality and love. They seem to be irreducible themselves; their concrete relationship with other things is not apparent. It is hard even to sense that the way we feel towards each other (we as women, we as men, we as a class, or we as an epoch) is specific and determinate. It is hard not to think that everyone in all ages must have felt these 'human' feelings we feel; not to think that sex is a biologically given instinct, which provides basically the same kind of experience, but is only more or less suppressed in different societies.

Yet a feeling, just like an idea, can only be felt if the social relations which contain it, make it a possible feeling. It is not just the ideology of the age which is produced within the mode of production; the type of feeling is specific and bounded too. It is not just bourgeois ideology about love and sex, or bourgeois morality and conventions that sustain bourgeois sexual practice; it is the very structure of our most intimate and powerful perceptions, emotions and ways of acting.

Imagine how differently sex must be felt to connect with emotional and other attachments to people in a kinship society where sex is a matter for public initiation, deflowering an occasion for solemn communal rejoicing, a social act on behalf of the collective hope for fertility, not a private act of emotional commitment or sensual pleasure between two individuals.

It is not just the imagination that is tested. There is a guilty anxiety about dissecting a pattern of feeling as strong and as shaking as love in its romantic and idealising form. The social relations persist in which individual sex-love spontaneously arises, and hence also the ideology that idealises it as sacrosanct and unquestionable. We may feel it to be a more and more contradictory type of feeling, with an urgency to understand it. Yet the word 'love' has such moral reverberations that this project arouses resentment and suspicion; it is as if we were questioning human values as such, care for each other, commitment to one's sexuality to chosen people, solidarity and loyalty.

Even within the broad sexual liberation movement there is an ideology of spontaneity, of expressing one's feelings as an absolute value, which takes feelings as given, which trusts what we spontaneously feel as a basis for sexual change, as though it was the power of the feelings as such — whatever their nature — that would break down the social relations that structure sexuality. Really, the feelings and the structures go together within a certain range of variation. This spontaneist idea assumes that there is some area within us that entirely escapes being formed and coloured by the social relations of capitalism, and which have only to be released from their captivity somewhere within us.

So, one of our problems in creating a sexual politics is that perceptions and feelings we have feel natural, human, even eternal, as all capitalist relations do; and we are told that they are too. The oppressing structures of monogamy and various forms of 'permissiveness' within which these personal emotions are felt, make it impossible to become conscious of their specificity (their particularity to this social structure) as long as we remain living within them.

This makes it hard even to describe carefully the quality and contradictions experienced in our present and past lives, which is a pre-requisite for analysis. Yet this is what we have to begin to do if we are to work towards a concrete practice in the sexual struggle, if we are to have even the glimmerings of an idea of what a concrete practice which is socialised and not private, would be.

The knowledge we need cannot be gained by abstract thinking and studying, but only in the process of beginning to change the family-created structures and feelings in our own lives.

But it is not just in our own personal lives that there are real contradictions necessitating a politics of sexuality. There are several indications that the personal relationships of working class women are under real strains at the present time. Urban redevelopment has meant that old communities have been up-rooted, and with them the supportive network of female relatives that many women depended on, so that on the new estates, in the flats tailor-made for individualised nuclear families, the conjugal relationship has had to bear the full brunt of emotional life in a way it never used to. The mental hospitals and doctors' surgeries are full of women – and mainly working class women – who have had nervous breakdowns or who are carrying on only because of anti-depressant pills such as valium.

Contraception and moves towards equal pay have given working class women at least a vision of an independent life, which puts emotional relationships of the traditional structure under greater strain. There are increasing numbers of broken marriages, and countless women are just fed up with the meaninglessness of their lives and their relationships. While it is true that in many ways the family and the relationships within it, provide an escape from the horrors of work, at the same time, it is often the case that work, and the relationships between workmates, offer an escape from the horrors of the family.

Most of us have found that we have needed to make changes in our own emotional relationships. But that has not been an easy thing to do. Unless we can make public a political understanding of what we have been struggling for in our own personal lives, we can only appear arrogant and really elitist in our attitudes towards working class women — as though we were being moralistic, saying that women 'should' want to be independent, instead of making it clear that we too have contradictory feelings, with real needs for emotional security. And unless we have a strategy for confronting these questions directly, we will never be able to wage a successful struggle against those aspects of family life that are now inextricably bound up with the emotional relationships within it — such as individualised domestic work, or the perpetual striving for material goods for the home.

SEXUAL POLITICS AND THE WOMEN'S MOVEMENT

As marxists and feminists, we have some general ideas about the relationships between sexism, the monogamous couple and capitalist relations of production. But to take seriously that the personal is political, we cannot remain content with attacking sexism and male chauvinism in the outside world. We have to understand the exact bonds which unite the couple, and to begin the long struggle of changing the ways we have been formed into monogamous, coupular women. And most importantly, we must recognise that these 'private' struggles are a major part of the struggle against sexism and integral to the political practice of the women's movement.

The women's movement is engaged in many forms of struggle against sexism: campaigns and demands for nurseries; control of our bodies; making contact with working class women through unions, tenants' associations, women's centres; attacking male chauvinism at many levels, in the Miss World contest as well as within left-wing groups. The sexual struggle within relationships occurs alongside these. Many of us are involved in heterosexual emotional relationships, and, if so, the attempt to begin changing the structures of our relationships and ways of feeling probably is being carried out in our own lives, on the basis of the felt contradictions in existing relationships. What the struggle will actually entail for any individual obviously cannot be prescribed. It may entail getting uncoupled, relating to several people emotionally, becoming gay, or becoming celibate. But insofar as any of these courses of action are part of the general struggle against sexism, we should be prepared to make them public.

For many women, these struggles will in fact involve men, and we must share our knowledge of what we are trying to do, rather than feeling guilty about that and keeping quiet. Consciousness raising groups have been one of the forms in which our private sexual struggles have been communicated between us. But they cannot in themselves change emotional relationships, if the struggle within these is not usually conducted within such groups themselves. This is not to deny the value of consciousness raising groups or the autonomy of the movement, but to emphasise that the political practice of the movement is linked with the outside, and with the reality of heterosexual relationships.

Indeed, one of the greatest achievements of the women's movement so far has been to challenge the division between public and private life imposed by bourgeois society, and to show that personal relationships are social and political. In consciousness raising groups, many women have learnt that their 'personal' problems are general female characteristics and socially determined, rather than individual failings, and this in itself opened up the possibility of change. Consciousness raising was a double process: not just a method of getting to know more about the social conditions of women, but also an intervention in our own lives. When we had talked openly to other women, we would be better equipped to resist domination by men, and eventually to make concrete changes in our relationships to men and to women.

But the knowledge gained in consciousness raising groups has largely been kept within them, and has not been made collective knowledge for the movement. We can see that many women have changed the formal basis of their personal lives. But we hear about these changes through rumours, in a gossipy way, now and then. We don't know how these changes are understood by the people involved, what they amount to in practice, or whether they arose out of consciousness raising.

How, concretely, are we living? What have we all been learning in the process of changes we have consciously attempted or which have happened to us reluctantly? As a movement we don't know. There has not been a socialisation of the struggle, and so the privacy and the incommunicability which bourgeois society imposes on sexual relationships has been reproduced unwittingly by us. If we regard these, at present, private aspects of our lives as an essential part of the theorising about the family and sexuality, we have to find ways of making public our understandings of the way we are trying to change. Maybe the women who write theoretically about sexism and the family have a critical political relationship towards their own sexual practice, and in fact may have drawn lessons from it. But none of that gets explicitly said, with the result that what appears in written form is abstract and mystifying: as such it reproduces male ways of theorising by not making clear the concrete basis on which the ideas were thought up, so they appear intimidatingly to be the emanation of a super-clever (female) individual brain.

Here is an example of the kind of experience that one of us had from being in a consciousness raising group for over a year. We don't know how representative it is:

"In my consciousness raising group we took a theme each week, like not having an identity, insecurity, relationships with our fathers, ideas about love, and each discussed our experience of these things. At first, we found a lot of basic similarities between us. But as time went on, we became so concerned about preserving the solidarity of the group, and about having the same female character-structure, that we found it very difficult to admit to any differences between us, because they were implicitly thought of as disruptive of the group.

We also failed to discuss in any detail our ongoing emotional relationships with men, or sex, and most of us did not really know who was relating to men and in what ways. So, what went on in the group was removed from people's actual sexual relationships and it was unclear how our discoveries and knowledge of ourselves was being used in practice. Part of the reason for this was the feeling that to talk about relationships with men constituted a betrayal of the women in the group who weren't with men, even though most were in fact relating to men. However, none of this was ever discussed openly: it was as though our private lives were being conducted in isolation from the things we said about men in the group."

UNDERSTANDING THE PAST TO CHANGE THE PRESENT

In our group now, each of us is involved in emotional-sexual relationships with someone in the group, if not only within it. So, talking about ourselves has been directly related to what we are trying to achieve politically within our relationships. For several months, one of the activities of the group has been to tell each other our 'life histories'. We have tried to give an account to each other, as we never had done to ourselves, of our formation, sexual as well as emotional, and also educational and political. We tried to see how our sexual and emotional formation was connected with the other aspects of our own formation because normally they feel disconnected. This meant looking at how schools affected sexuality, as well as performing their explicit function of intellectual formation, and looking at families to see how they affected intellectual formation in relation to the emotional bonds within them. This included giving accounts of the present, and not just looking backwards into the past.

The intellectual formation of each person clearly has an effect on the whole way we have of talking, and to expose the roots of these ways in the past was part of the attempt at mutual de-mystification necessary to working and talking collectively. Likewise, the sexual-emotional formation of each of us was directly involved in an understanding of what was going on in present relationships, because it is impossible to say things to other people about your own sexual experience and feelings without having a definite idea of the resonances it will have for them. We had to try to understand the material and social basis of what we were doing in our present relationships, not in some general abstract way, but with a real grasp of the particularity of each person.

The aim of telling the life histories, therefore, was to start with a particular and practical knowledge of the contradictions felt by each of us, and to develop a theoretical understanding of the interconnections between our sexual, intellectual, political and economic lives. We all felt it

13

was not principally ideas about sexual politics that had influenced us, so much as the developing dynamic of past and present relationships, even the ways we had been changed unconsciously. We also wanted to know how much we might have been repeating past patterns of relating, so that changing really meant changing, and not just a turnover of personnel.

Trying to build a theory on the particular contradictions felt and the particular practices pursued by each of us within the group is intended to avoid the possibility of just trying to change, in a voluntaristic or moralistic way, and of imposing any models on other people, such as simply ruling out jealousy as an illegitimate feeling which no good revolutionary ought to feel. If jealousy has a real basis in the past and in the present structures and forms of feelings, we had to grasp what these were, and to see if there were contradictions which could be a real basis for wanting to change. One result is that we cannot say that we think the contradictions we, a small bunch of university educated women and men, have detected, are at all general. Indeed, the women's movement has shown that because of women's particular relations to personal relationships, the contradictions are in general much more acutely felt by women. But it is only on the basis of starting to understand and theorise real, but particular contradictions, that we can begin to get some idea of what we are trying to do, and finding out what others are trying to do.

We have all found it very difficult to talk, let alone to write, about ourselves in an objective manner. Writing about oneself seems still to be like a personal and individual thing to do, even if it isn't intended as such. On the one side, it seems it could be a possible exhibition, open to exposure and attack; on the other, it seems like claiming to be somebody special, or to have achieved something special — which is not the case. We have been in situations which have made it imperative for each of us to understand our relationships. It is because such situations do have such a personal importance and centrality in our lives — even, from a marxist or feminist position, in spite of ourselves — that such a going over of our life histories has become a political activity of our group. We think that this kind of concrete knowledge has to become part of a knowledge of a general political movement, which is the only way of making the particular and concrete general — there are no short cuts.

You will see, from these four examples of life-histories which follow, that each of us had emphasised different aspects, using different styles and moods. We have all abstracted out in a one-sided way, our emotional and sexual life histories. We don't really know how to write about ourselves in a way that does communicate to others the contradictions which we have each felt, so to help form the basis of a general sexual politics.

FOUR LIFE HISTORIES

A woman   "Throughout my life there has been only one person with
whom I have had a very close emotional relationship, and that is the man
whom I met at school, was living with at 18, and had married at 20. And
that relationship was one in which I unconsciously but actively submerged
myself, my interests, my ideas, and my identity, and became more and
more incapable of engaging in any activity or relating to anybody else at
all.

My parents' relationship to each other, and to me, and all the
relationships within the family were characterised by their lack of
emotional content. My parents didn't 'love' each other, but they didn't
have flaming rows either. They lived in the same house, did some things
together, but a lot of things separately, and generally got on each other's
nerves. I'm sure they had no on-going sexual relationship; they taught me
about sex as a way of producing babies, but nothing — explicitly or
implicitly — about sexuality or sexual love. My mother was constantly
criticising in a mocking, sarcastic way, my father's absent-mindedness, and
general lack of competence at dealing with the everyday practicalities of
life or remembering simple facts. Throughout my late childhood and teens,
I completely supported my mother in her attacks on my father, and
identified with her view of him. I respected him for his academic work and
his knowledge of political affairs, and I would discuss these with him
sometimes, but I had a real contempt for his stupidity, clumsiness and
forgetfulness.

But although I identified with my mother vis-a-vis my father, I did
not have a close relationship with her. She was always very reserved and
cool, and above all, competent and efficient in everything. From a fairly
early age, I was made aware of being like her; in contrast to my father, I
was observant, practical and resourceful. I was allowed to be independent
of them in many ways, and I grew up despising not only the absent-
minded type of 'not coping' that my father epitomised, but also the

15

neurotic, weak, emotional type of 'not coping' that I saw in a lot of women — the female character really.

I have two brothers but no sisters, and I never had any long lasting or deep friendships with any girls during my childhood or teens. There was nobody with whom I ever discussed emotional problems or experiences, and I used to find all display of strong feelings very embarrassing — e.g. if a friend was crying I wouldn't know how to react, because her feelings would seem completely foreign to me.

I did feel isolated and sometimes very lonely, especially during my late teens, and I was conscious of finding it very difficult to develop friendships, but at the same time, my desire to cope created a sense of self-sufficiency, entailing a great intolerance of other people, particularly girls, I think.

So from fairly early on in my relationship with X, he was important to me not just as a boyfriend, but as a 'best friend'. Originally, there were quite substantial differences between us, in terms of interests and also of our politics, but we both changed a lot over the first year that we knew each other, and together we started to learn about socialist politics in the wake of the student movement. The changes that X underwent during this time were much more fundamental than they were for me, and I got into university a year before he did. So our relationship started on a basis in which I was the one leading the way really, knowing more about the things we were both trying to find out about, having read more of the books we were interested in, and getting to university first.

I felt quite uncomfortable about this at the time — it seemed wrong somehow. It created a situation in which X idealised me I think, or at least I felt idealised and uneasy about whether I really lived up to the ideal. I wanted to develop my own interests in and knowledge of Marxism, etc., but at the same time I was so anxious that he should come to know about it all himself, and develop into someone I could look up to in admiration — as I'd admired aspects of my father — that from an early stage, certainly by the time I went to university and he came to live with me there, I would just not read anything around a particular topic, so that I never read any Lenin for example. Once we were living together we started to build up a respectable Marxist library, but soon I left all the buying of books to him, and so the situation developed in which I didn't even know what we had, or what half the books were about.

But the strange thing about this was that neither X nor I were conscious of this happening at the time, and I've only been able to think about it now, in the last year or so. Although X gradually started discussing politics etc., much less with me than with some of his friends (men) — while I would sit and listen or (honestly!) be out in the kitchen cooking — I never consciously realised that I wasn't joining in. I never thought about myself as the person who hadn't read *'Imperialism'* or knew

16

almost nothing about the labour theory of value. This wasn't because X would explain everything to me—he didn't much. I thought of myself as knowing about these things, just because he did, and because my identity was so bound up with his that I couldn't really distinguish between the two. This was until I eventually became involved in political activity independently of him, when it hit me like a bombshell that I, me, in my own right, wasn't what I'd believed myself to be.

It had been very important to me that we were the kind of couple who, in contrast to my parents, did everything together and agreed on everything. Any differences seemed to me to threaten our close emotional relationship, and the most effective way for me to avoid this was in fact for me not to get involved in anything myself, and not to develop any kind of 'line' of my own, but to adopt X's. In activities in which we were involved, such as a squatting campaign, I cannot remember a single difference on tactics or strategy arising between me and him — which is surely not something one could say about anyone else with whom one was working politically. I later became increasingly withdrawn from people generally, and less and less involved in political activity. But I still cherished the idea of myself as a political person — an idea which was based purely on my identity within the relationship, which I regarded as a kind of political partnership. X was involved in activity at his university, and he knew all the theory, so that was enough.

From when I first went to university, I was completely torn between on the one hand wanting to get to know people, and get involved in political activities, and on the other, the relationship with X was external to all that and acting as a pull in the opposite direction. I found it impossible to be active not because X discouraged me or anything, but because of the structure of the relationship. What is perfectly easy for a man — and in fact some of the male left have wives sitting at home and giving them moral and emotional support in their work — put really conflicting pressures on me. This was partly because the men expected all new women coming on the scene to be generally sexually available. I wasn't and I didn't know how to make this clear without withdrawing altogether. But also my relation with X had become established on such an exclusive basis — with me having no other close friends — that I found it difficult to get in any way involved with other people. Because I had this relationship with X, I had had no need to change the way I related to other people.

In fact, I had become even more distanced from and intolerant of those around me, because he could confirm the feelings I had about them — he was an ally in the world, which meant that I didn't have to think about how I should change, but only what was wrong with others. Actually I had ambivalent feelings about this, as I'd believed for a long time that I was going to meet wonderful people at university, and I wanted to make friends. But these conflicts quickly exploded when the first interesting and nice person that I met wanted to go to bed with me. X was very upset, and although I was very confused, I was basically frightened of the unknown, of being on my own again, and of losing the only person I'd been close to.

So, I gave in, and that's how I experienced it — me surrendering, and submerging myself even more deeply into the relationship, and feeling guilty for having attacked it, while at the same time getting a lot of satisfaction from behaving in this way, atoning from my sins, showing how much I was prepared to sacrifice, and seeing X really appreciative of this, being grateful and loving. It was at this time that I also started cooking for him and washing his shirts, not because I thought I ought to, but because it was another expression of self-sacrificing love. I became increasingly withdrawn from others; the only people I really got to know were people we both knew, and who knew us as a couple.

I had another short-lived 'affair' which led to the same sequence of events as before, with X threatening to leave me, and then tormented by remorse, shame and a desperate need to prove to him that I really did love him. Afterwards, when it was all patched up, and I was busy cooking even bigger and better meals, I couldn't think about what had happened at all, or understand anything about why I should suddenly burst out of my self-denying, self-sacrificing existence with a burst of selfish deceit and aggression towards X. I just kept apologising.

What changed things for me was moving to London after I finished university. For, here I became completely dependent on X for all social contacts with the outside world in a way I had never been before. He had friends and activities centred around his university, but I knew nobody, was unemployed, had nothing to do. I was very miserable and realised that I had to get involved in some activity in my own right, and get to know some people independently of X.

I eventually forced myself out into working in community politics. I began working closely with people who knew me as myself not as half a couple, and it was only then that I became conscious of the difficulties I had in relating to other people, because I no longer wanted to withdraw from them. I wanted to get to know people better, but I felt really clamped up inside, frightened of anyone getting too close or behaving in an emotional way. I didn't feel I could relate to people openly, when it often felt as though the other half of me wasn't there. I would be out doing things all day or all evening with others, but would always return home to X. When I did get involved in a sexual relationship with Y, my life became completely compartmentalised. I was always either with X or with Y, each making incompatible demands on me, but at different times and places, so that when I was with X, I could never clearly remember what I had thought or said or felt whan I was with Y, and vice versa. I was in an impossible situation, I couldn't move. I couldn't think of giving up my relationship with Y because that seemed to mean giving up the whole of my independent activity and returning to things as they were. I did try this for a while, but I could no longer be contented with the old masochistic, self-sacrificing role.

On the other hand, to leave X seemed inconceivable. To split seemed like splitting myself in two; there were so many things I couldn't imagine doing separately. I became completely confused, and therefore with X and with Y, I acted in a passive, indecisive, manner, letting each of them take the initiative, make decisions, and set out demands from me instead of thinking of what I wanted to do myself.

I had found myself not knowing what my feelings were, wondering if I had any feelings at all. I wasn't thinking rationally about my situation and what I wanted to do, but emotionally I thought only of myself, and was quite unable to understand either X's or Y's needs or feelings. In particular, because my relationship with Y was established against the background of my relationship with X and the problem of what I was going to do about that, I never put very much effort into working out what was happening within the relationship with Y itself, only whether or not I should let it exist. I was using him as a safety-valve, and when he was no longer prepared to accept this, he was setting out conditions for our relationship which threatened the basis of my relationship with X, and its centrality in my life, in a way that it didn't before.

I couldn't cope with the consequences that this had, both for me, still having deep-seated fears about losing the secure base of the coupular relationship with X, and in terms of X's reaction. So, I couldn't continue with the relationship with Y at that time, but I had learnt too much and experienced too much of the other side of my contradictory feelings for me to remain in the couple for much longer. I knew I had to sort out the central problem – the relationship with X – as the only way of coming to terms with the continuing difficulties I was having in relating to other people, particularly the people I was working with.

We are now living separately, but we are still having a relationship, trying to put it on a new basis, so that we no longer function as a couple. For me, this entails attempting to take control over my situation in my personal life, rather than being sewpt along either by my unconscious needs and desires to be self-denying and submissive, or, through my own passivity, by the initiative of men I am involved with. It means thinking seriously about myself, and trying to understand my contradictory, ambivalent feelings instead of being immobilised by my confusion."

A woman   "Until recently, I had made very contradictory demands of emotional relationships. On the one hand, feeling very insecure and alone in the world, I wanted to be very close to someone, but I also wanted to be completely alright on my own, able to manage without whatever emotional relationships I was in fact in.

In practice this entailed all sorts of rituals to prove to myself I could manage without X, and then resenting him for being there at all, but on the other hand wanting him there as a background, and feeling rejected by him. A sort of real contradiction between neurotic dependency and insecurity, and a desire for complete equanimity and independence from any emotional involvement. So I wanted to be involved emotionally but as soon as I was, I resented it as a drain on myself. I experienced having feelings as oppressive and weakening, but also the thing I was most frightened of was being on my own. I only came to realise this sort of conflict when I started re-enacting the whole pattern with another man, and found that I couldn't get close to anyone even if I wanted to, because of all the internal barriers and fears. I was convinced that ultimately I was going to be on my own anyhow, so that I had better start getting used to it now, and not get close to anyone because it would be even harder when it finished.

The main thing about this pattern was the conflict between dependence and independence. We know that love relationships can be very debilitating, and establish a sort of common personality between two people which drags the woman down more than the man as she lives more of her life through emotional relationships. But my relationship with X was not of this romantic love variety: for the reasons given, it was on a somewhat subdued and contradictory emotional key. So my fear of involvement wasn't a feminist reaction to an oppressive love relation at all. In fact I'd had this horror of emotional involvement for ages: at 15 or 16 I decided that I would never get married, that instead I would have an independent career and a series of affairs but I'd never settle down with any one person. I liked the idea of being a single woman and having relationships that lasted for a few months. On the other hand, this dream was completely unrealistic given my fear of being on my own, and what in fact happened was that I met X when I was 17, and lived with him for five years from when I was 20. All the time we lived together we pretended that we were independent entities (never shared money or possessions) and I was continually trying to prove to myself that I could manage without him, which he realised, but which we never spoke about. This situation was able to continue for such a long time partly because we lived with other people, and never on our own, as a couple.

This precocious aversion to marriage which was really an aversion to any emotional involvement was only feminist in a contradictory way. I didn't want to become the stereotype of a woman, and I had a real horror of housewives, mothers and happy families. I wanted to be like a man, only unmarried, and I thought that being a housewife or a mother with small children was the most awful thing in the world that could happen to me. I really despised women as a teenager, but had no understanding of how they were forced to lead the kinds of lives they led. All this meant that I had a very ambiguous relationship with girlfriends who were good at doing female things like sewing or who knew a lot about make-up — they would treat me as blue-stockingy, uninterested in such things, and I found that I could talk much more easily to men about 'serious' matters, partly because women didn't take me seriously. (No doubt the men didn't either . . .)

This might sound as if I behave in a very 'mature' or male way, but I don't at all; my main mode which fits with that fear of getting involved or revealing myself, is cheeky and rather childlike. I hope I'm getting over this now, but what used to happen was that as soon as I experienced any feelings for some one, I'd suddenly start behaving in a very ludic way, playing at being emotionally involved or sexy, rather than expressing what I felt, so that I wouldn't have to risk my 'real self'. This entailed a lot of symbolic and ritualistic gestures, as I was far too embarrassed to show what I was really feeling for fear of exposure and eventual rejection. So I'd be affectionate and playful with men as I had been with my father, just acting towards the other person but unable to respond to any move he made towards me, even if I wanted to. So rather than entering into a relationship where interaction occurred between people, I would always prevent this from starting by acting in a childlike and alienated way. I can see how the whole thing fits together now, from having tried to change it, but this has been a long process and depended on constructing a relationship that wasn't based on that choice between dependence and independence. Before, I just knew that I was afraid of being on my own, and of being emotionally involved.

In my case, this conflict seems to be the result of what my parents did to me, and due to my contradictory socialisation rather than what men did to me. My parents are Jewish refugees and professional people, scientists. My mother is extremely ambitious career-wise, and has a much stronger version of this contempt for women than I ever had. I was the only child, not really wanted but the apple of the eye once there. My mother resented the child for interfering with her work and I was always looked after by other people as a child. My father had not wanted a child at all. However they had great ambitions for me and as a small child I knew I was going to university and that the only thing that really mattered was schoolwork. They poured contempt on my friends' mothers who didn't work, and in fact on women generally, and on anyone who wasn't intellectual. Their glorification of academics and of intelligence as such (inherited of course) was one of the mystifications they used to control me with.

Everything I did was caused by having either my mother's or

father's genes, and this includes things like being good at wrapping up Xmas presents (my father's genes) or leaving food on my plate (my (mother's). Their genetic determinism was a means of making me into an extension of them: everything I did that they approved of showed that I was their child, and everything they disliked was immediately invalidated, and I was told I was stupid or just ignored. So I learned not to express any thought I did have because I knew it would be attacked. This carried on after I left 'home' and I still find it very difficult to disagree with people openly. They were always wanting me to perform, and to prove myself as a reincarnation of them. They would quarrel over me too, each wanting me to be more like them than the other. When I eventually expressed political views, these were dismissed on the grounds that they were what other people thought, and I didn't really think them because my parents didn't. They were incapable of treating me in any sense as an independent person.

They also tied me to them emotionally in a very screwy way. They never took any notice of what I felt, but behaved just as they liked towards me, and expected unconditional love in return. My mother was quite open about wanting a child so that someone would love her, and while she used to treat it as a real favour to me if she was at home when I got back from school, she would expect me to kiss and cuddle her whenever she demanded it. That was partly how I learned to put on those shows of affection. My parents still demand affection in a completely symbolic way ('go and kiss your mother to show how much you love her') and don't express any real emotions. This goes along with being very rationalistic, which I'll explain in a bit. Anyway, my mother was always accusing me as a child of loving the women she employed to look after me more than her, which I did.

Another aspect of this was their view of the family as the only reliable domestic unit, and relationships between parents and children as much more stable than those between spouses. They didn't want me to have boyfriends because it would take me away from them, and I was told that they were more dependable than a man would ever be. My mother encouraged me not to get married, and to sleep around, and she was relieved when X and I lived together rather than getting married. They didn't think the relationship would last long though, as I was more intelligent than him. When he and I eventually split up, my mother told me how insecure I was, and how they both worried about what would happen to me when they died as I was 'so bad at making friends'. A classical double bind.

A final point about their ideology. Their biologism and aversion to emotions had a great effect on my sexual formation. At 4, I knew where babies came from, how sperms got in and how the baby came out. All this was explained as a purely biological process — I had no idea why people had sex. Similarly the body was treated as something you had that did things, and that things came out of, and that grew things that had to be seen to and kept clean. If anyone was irritable it was always because they were having their periods (men being moody was OK), and I developed a real mind/body split in which I felt like a thing trapped in a body that wasn't really part of me. But as I was only a body if I looked in a mirror, I couldn't work out who I was, the thing inside or the body I could see. I didn't want to grow up because that meant growing breasts, having periods and turning into a woman, which was the last thing I wanted to be. So as an adolescent I continued to act like a child, and this was welcomed in the context, because my parents wanted me to remain a child too.

What I want to make clear is that as a child I had to defend myself against my parents' 'love', and did this by withdrawing and trying not to express any feelings or ideas. I was always terrified of what would happen to me if they died, and didn't want to be left on my own because I felt very insecure without them. But I also wanted to be alright on my own and to enjoy myself without them being there. I resented them for making me lonely by not being there. And this is the root of the independence/ dependence conflict which I took with me from them into my adult relationships. It is also the root of not being able to express myself emotionally: they thought that emotions were a sign of immaturity, and there was no point expressing anything I felt to them as it would be either invalidated or incorporated. Also I thought that to express being upset or liking someone was a revelation of something that would be used against me, and that I should be embarrassed and ashamed of having feelings coming out of me. Romantic emotions were treated as a joke by my parents and derided, and whenever they expressed any affection, it was always in a childish and symbolic way, a big kiss on the cheek or a tickle at the back of the neck. Their whole way of thinking made me not want to be a women because they were stupid and more bodies than anything else.

The effect of all this is that my problem has not been that of stopping falling in love or having the feelings that drag women down or make them subservient to men, but that of daring to express what I think or feel, to be able to accept emotional involvement, and to overcome embarrassment and shame at my own body."

A woman "I've picked out one particular strand in my life history: why is it that although I have not been confined by the material conditions which are understood to oppress women (housework, educational superiority of the man, economic dependence of the woman, children), I have still felt very contained within the personal by my relationships with men?·

I have had all the advantages of emancipation; yet since I was 18, my most consistent preoccupations have been within love for a man. I was educated with the most elite of men until I was 24, and I'm not afraid of men in general; yet I still feel timid and panic-stricken in comparison with the man I'm in love with. My conscious priority has always been for a political working life. I was never to marry, I said at 17, never to be confined to the private, condemned to the personal, like my mother. Yet at 19 I was married, and at 26 I was feeling my activities in the outside world had become progressively stunted by anxieties about what the man I had lived with since I was 21, thought about me. I can see that the activity and knowledge of most of the men I was educated with is deformed and brutalised by being monopolised by them against other men and women for their exploitation and humiliation; yet I feel nervous and judged, sometimes afraid to think my own thoughts in the face of the competence and conviction of the man I'm in love with, who is a comrade.

It has been the contradictions and ambivalences of the love relationship which have infiltrated all other aspects of my life, including attempts to act and think within the Women's Liberation movement. He was always there as an absent presence to whom I referred myself.

Why do I say that love is ambivalent? Because I love him and resent him. I am scared if he turns his gaze away from me, but I defend myself from him by secrecy and silences. I depend on his absorption in me, but I am always on the edge of escaping from him. I fear for him, the hero-man, the vulnerable individual in his projects, and I fear him, his competence, his confidence. I think he will always love me for who I am, but I expect that at any moment he will despise me for what I do, I feel, almost superstitiously, that my only salvation lies in loving and being loved.

But we thought we were comrades, equals (the man I lived with after marriage). We were going to live together, work together. That's how it began. It was he who wished it too (in contrast to my husband, who had explicitly anti-feminist, male supremacist ideas). Like many of our men, he too was frustrated and nonplussed by my losses of confidence and despairing feelings of uselessness and inadequacy. We both wanted us to be co-workers, only it didn't work.

A pattern was set up between us, in which I loved him, but thought he would reject me if I didn't live up to his high ideal of me. For it isn't that I felt that I wasn't loved enough, nor that I didn't love him enough. I haven't had to face real concrete uncertainties or insecurities in case he would leave me or didn't really love me. On the contrary it was idealising love that we had for each other that made me in awe of him, and also feel I would disapppoint his ideal of me. In the absence of any signs of contempt from him, still the constant presence of what I felt to be his ideal-image of me, created the intimation of its potential opposite, contempt, which I had to guard myself against. Sometimes, though, I just felt relief in having my identity secured by his gaze. Gradually anxieties about his judgement of me outweighed this.

All this was complicated, and the feelings made more intractable and hard to think about, because of the way that sex fitted into the pattern between us. Two or three times during the years, I had a short and disruptive sexual relationship with other people, which set up resentful anxiety on his part, resentful guilt on mine. I could never talk about it properly, because I had no rational explanation for my actions, which I now interpret as subversive action against the couple we were, which I had to act against indirectly, because I couldn't formulate any critical thoughts about it.

This set up a particularly paralysing combination of feelings: guilt for hurting him, and especially for not being able to give a proper explanation or reasons, which made it look like completely irresponsible and careless action; and yet a kind of unverbalised (to myself) subterranean conviction that I hadn't been wrong in what I had done. I responded overtly to the first feeling, atoning for the infidelities and being very apologetic; but the other knowledge remained, stored up as inarticulate resentment that surfaced every now and again.

My placatory stance, and his now strong need for sexual reassurance, made sex, which had before been symbolic for the love, become symbolic of my return to him. That meant that I couldn't help feeling that making love was a confirmation that I had been in the wrong and had to make it up, and so I became very resistant to sex. This was a way of expressing indirectly the same ambivalence contained in my apologies. I would make love, but coldly. This was not under my control. I would really want to be warm and sexual with him, but as soon as we started I would get tense and anxious, so he would be hurt and defeated. I would make my recompense, but had my revenge, all unconsciously.

The articulation of sex with the emotional deadlock in this way, meant that practical sexual difficulties became impossible to talk about. We hadn't talked about sex before because, since it was supposed to be expressive of our love (for me, anyway), it would have been love that seemed under attack if anything were admitted to be imperfect about sex. Now that we were at bay emotionally, suspicious of each other, with all the resentments that are the converse of love very close to the surface, this kind of process was even worse: I couldn't even think about sex between us because it made me so worried and anxious: I put it out of my mind. So sex became a divisive thing between us in its own right, though sex as such hadn't been the cause of it. For a long time, I didn't have any understanding at all of the cause of this impasse. The cycles never seemed to end. Every attempt to work it out ended in knots.

The ideas I had about us as a couple were, throughout this time, amazingly idealistic. I didn't have any criticisms of us, only of myself. I couldn't have talked to anyone in my women's group, because I was so loyal to the idea of us as a loving and comradely couple that I couldn't even think critical thoughts to myself. But at the same time, I did know at some level that there was something wrong with the emotional basis of the relationship. It's hard to explain the sense in which I knew this. It took the form of an uneasiness in talking about sexual politics, a defensiveness in talking about anything personal to other people, and a great block about thinking about myself. I just took apparently irrational, because untheorised, actions against the relationship, and quietly, unintentionally, sabotaged it in sex, which naturally enough exasperated him.

Meanwhile: for a good three years of this relationship I was active in the women's movement. I had a formal commitment to the idea of a politics of the personal, and I did some theoretical study on the family in capitalism, but I couldn't utter an authentic word about my own personal life. The most threatening things to think about were anything to do with the lived experience of the family: love itself, sexuality, the monogamous couple. To think critically about these things I would have had to disengage from total identification with this man and with 'us', in order to hold us up to the light. The guilt and anxiety and panic generated by the love relationship made that very hard to do as long as I was within it.

Another thought-stopper was the fact that the man himself isn't a male chauvinist at all, and that bemused me. My logic was that since he wasn't oppressing me with any reactionary or tyrannical habits and attitudes of his, and I had none of the material ties to him that would objectively oppress me, and my own upbringing had not emphasised my feminine role, it must be up to me, by a great effort of will and turning over a new leaves, to be 'sensible', 'get down to work', etc.. Since a lot of women's liberation talk seemed to be about much more individually reactionary men than he is, I thought it didn't apply to us. I thought I was a women who was screwed up and dependent in typical female ways. My ways of loving (not ours) made me colonised and passive.

He used to beg me to tell him what he did that oppressed me, and I couldn't think of anything. I knew his method of intellectual work and his verbalisations of everything intimidated and silenced me; but since it seemed to come out of his interest and enthusiasm, it seemed mean to say anything about that. (Looking back I can see that this kind of intellectuality, even if the person, usually the man, wishes to work with others rather than individualistically, does tend towards individualistic projects despite his intentions, and tends towards trying to incorporate all other intellectual endeavours and is of its nature competitive when it is thinking unconnected with a practice that collectivises people. This is as true of my abstracted intellectuality as his, being academically educated too; good intentions aren't enough to avoid this.)

My logic left me flailing about within the relationship, not sure who was to blame. I didn't manage to think it was the relationship between us, its emotional basis and exclusiveness, its centrality, that made us feel in infantile ways. If two people decide to be everything to each other, they have reproduced the childhood relationships to the parents, and as in that infantile relation, the demands for total love, the panic at loss, the impossibility of coping with hostility, the mixture of love with aggression and awe, arise despite oneself. My logic missed the possibility that even though he was not an oppressor to blame for my misery, the love relationship would still have to be abandoned in its present form and quality.

I didn't understand that there is a dialectical relationship between the man's gain and the woman's loss in a love relationship. When I left for short periods during the years we were together and when we finally separated, it was he who was laid low, anxious and panic-stricken, feeling the loss of confidence and conviction that I had felt when we were together. A man doesn't have to be a Victorian patriarch like Torvald in *The Doll's House* for his woman to wilt, and he to draw his strength from her.

It is the dilemma of antisexist men who could be our comrades that the emotional support they draw from the women they love is necessary to them. Individualism is a project that has rarely been carried out fully: every man's work has needed a context of encouragement and interest. And the less there are any other structures of relationships to give solidarity, the more people are forced into the isolation of couples to sustain each other's efforts, which in practice means sustaining the man's.

It was not anything I read or talked about in the women's movement that eventually forced me to think about the love relationship critically. Instead, it was a rather silly and humiliating experience: I 'fell in love' with someone who didn't want to love me. I refused to register this fact for a long time, which meant that my feelings were being directed towards someone who was hardly interacting with me at all (though I sometimes thought he was, since he was master of the ambiguous message). The obsessiveness of my feelings for him began to seem mad: how could I be feeling all this, with all the disruption of my work that went along with it, for no return? It seemed like events only in my head. The person who was the object of all this affection was practically oblivious to its existence, so what was this affection? I realised that it was in my head, in one sense: much of the content of love is wish-projection. If the love is reciprocated, you don't see this. It is revealed when the love is one-sided, since no amount of coolness, rejection and nastiness could lessen the obsession with a man I hardly knew and had no real ties with.

This convinced me, after a long time wasted, that I must stop thinking the solution to my problems lay in just making resolutions to stop being so affected by my relationships with men, to be sensible (like a man), to throw myself into work, irrespective of what it was, to get absorbed in something that wasn't 'personal'. Since the politics I was wanting to work in was women's politics, this kind of repressive solution became a nonsense. The problem had to be tackled head on. My containment and thwarting by my sexual life was what had to be understood and made a subject for political change, not evasively dismissed as secondary. Hopefully, if I could understand the dynamics of this process in my life it might throw some light on the general conditions which oppress women."

A man   "I want to concentrate on just one aspect of my formation, and I will only deal with that in a very schematic way.

I lived in a particularly closed family. One of three brothers, I had very few friends, who never, or very rarely, came home. In this way, I related to people who were just already there, part of the family, and it can't really be said that I formed relationships at all. There was a kind of emotional pressure that made all friends outsiders, and their presence an attack on the emotional self-sufficiency of the family. My parents too had very few friends, and although that was not something I noticed, I did gradually become aware of it as I was distancing myself from the family, when it seemed to be an effect of some impasse in the relationship between my parents.

In this context, there was no possibility but that my emotions were centred around a reciprocation of mother-love, and less saliently, brotherly and fatherly feelings. I was close to my mother right through to 16 or 17, although I did everything with my brothers in a way which was more practical and game playing, without any real communication or revelation of deeply felt feelings

There was no room for sexuality, of course; either at home or at an all-boys school. The school-boy sexuality was one that just left me feeling totally anxious: it was a kind of contest basically going on between boys, but over girls: sex with the boys as it were. Emotional relations were formed in exclusion from any possible sexuality — parental sexuality was split off, and totally hidden. Sex was something unthinkable about within this context, there in physiological development, not there in any social expression. Emotionality was contained within the family, there being no real bonds with anyone outside. Consequently I devoted myself to thought, intellectual work, in order to defend myself against the unthinkable. I always used the excuse of the amount of work I had to do as a means of not having anything to do with anyone. In a way I could not have anything to do with anyone, because of the particularly totalitarian way in which emotional bonds were formed in relation to the given people of the family. So, this contradictory relation between the formation of emotions and paralysis of sex, an effect of a particular version of the nuclear family, meant that, on leaving the family, friendships appeared totally inadequate to this emotionality, and sexual relations impossible. I was in a kind of suspended existence — suspended between the family and nothing to replace it. All relationships to other people seemed superficial and pretty meaningless.

Out of this past came a monogamous love marriage. The state of meaninglessness could only be overcome within the context of me expressing equally totalitarian forms of love, which demanded reciprocation. I can't say that this emotion, coming from my family past, had anything to do with the woman it was imposed on, and it was an imposition. It took me a long time to realise that what was experienced as a powerfully positive feeling coming from me, could in fact be an imposition because it was unilateral, originating in my past and only expressing what I had been made emotionally capable of feeling, not based on any present relation.

Sex, in a sense, still had no place. The unthinkable remained largely unthinkable, and instead of trying to discover anything about sex as such, I was sexual only as a token, a symbolic expression of love. The way in which sex had been made unthinkable in the family, unconsciously, but as a part of my social emotional formation, was therefore reproduced in my marriage. Similarly, the way in which my love was totalitarian was totally unconscious, again an effect of the way in which the family had split, as a social relation, the outside of the family from the inside.

This incipient reproduction of the family broke down however. This was partly over sex, or rather over the relation between sex and love which had reduced sex to nothing in itself, a mere token of affection. This meant that sex was almost underground, untalked of, as in the family. It was as if the aim in sex was to find total emotional unity — which defies the sexual differences built into heterosexuality, or even the physical separateness and distinctness of two bodies. This was like trying not to be conscious of the separateness of each person through sex — having sex was like striving to reach a state of obliteration between two people, not just a question of being unselfconscious: all for emotional unification.

Partly the breakdown of the relationship was over the nature of the emotionality itself. For, my love demanded a total affirmation of myself. It was in showing that I could really love, that I could get an affirmation of my own identity (as well as being loved), so that I could then go on to do whatever I could in the outside world — much as anyone goes out from the family, the emotional base camp. I required that I should be affirmed as the person who loved by being loved back. But the way in which this was a unilateral demand coming out of my past made this, much in the same way as sex, an unrealistic project. It was such a negation of the other person (since it was not concretely based on a present relationship to a particular person) that it undermined her. Because of her different emotional formation, she did not have the responses to my totalitarian demands, and felt more of an absence of feeling in relation to it.

Because, as a consequence of my adolescent defences against sexuality, I had manufactured an identity as an intellectual, what occurred within the emotional relationship was far more a destruction of her than it was of me. The negation was that she could not feel what I, in a totalitarian feeling of love, was demanding of her, while at the same time she had no source of validation outside the relationship — my totalitarian demands for exclusiveness made sure of that. But the negation of her also had consequences for me. In the end the unreality of my sexual project and emotional demands meant that she was too negated to be an effective affirmer of my feelings for her. The unreality of my feelings in relation to the sense of how I had undermined her, gradually undermined those feelings themselves, not just towards her, but the capacity to feel those kinds of feelings. A lot of elements which I have not mentioned here entered into the break-up of this monogamous marriage, but I have wanted to trace through a threat of how my emotionality and sexuality was formed; and then subsequently transformed, unconsciously, in marriage.

The result of the break-up, however, was to lead to a completely disturbed relation between sexuality and emotionality. I was left totally emotionally (and, by the way, intellectually) confused about the relation between feelings and sex. This left me blocked and paralysed in the one relation I did have then which gradually ceased to be sexual because of the anxieties attached.

Such was the historical and material base, the kind of emotional and sexual contradictions, laid down by the family and then changed, which made some kind of politics of sexuality a felt necessity for me."

THEORY AND PRACTICE

The ideas that follow have been developed as we have tried to change our relationships; and in doing this we have worked out understandings of our past relationships, which we could not have had as we lived them. It will be very schematic, and does not amount to A Theory.

There are five of us in the group, three women and two men. Two of us (a man and a women) have been living together for several years, and are still having a relationship, but are no longer living together. The other two women are having a relationship with one man, also in the group. We have been trying to change three major aspects of our relationships, within the relationships each of us are in, and on the basis of the differences we each bring to it, as we've understood these from out life histories.

These three aspects which we would like to explain are: (1) Emotionality and sexuality; (2) Unconsciousness, consciousness and theory; (3) Structure of relationships. They are closely interrelated of course, and the linear way in which they are expressed is only a way of writing. They should each become clearer as successive ones are explained. Nor are these concepts the ones we started with in practice, of course. We gradually identified them as important in interaction with what we were actually doing in our relationships.

Emotionality and sexuality

We've tried to analyse the feelings characteristic of the couple and other personal relations under capitalism using four interlocking concepts.

Givenness of feelings

Feelings of love, liking, sexual attraction, are the main *raison d'etre* of personal relations under capitalism. Relationships are formed because people have feelings for each other. People act on the feelings that they take as givens, in the sense that these feelings are not felt to need explanation: you might be asked why you like or love a particular person, but not why you like or love as such. Sexual attraction is an example of givenness in this sense; so are the different ways that people combine their emotions with sexual attraction. Either you fancy someone or you don't; either you can enjoy sex with someone on the basis of sexual attraction alone, or you are the kind of person who only likes sex with someone you love and know very well. Feelings like this, and these differences between people, are taken as given — 'It's my personality'.

This is not to deny that there are other reasons than feelings and sexual attraction for a couple, say, to want to be together: often there are shared ideas and aspirations covering a lot of areas of work and politics as well. But it is still true to say that these relationships are based on given feelings, because it is these feelings which differentiate personal relationships of loving and liking from other relationships. The ideas and political work not only can be shared with others, but are actually mystified if it seems that they are shared only by two people owing to special qualities of mind and character.

The feelings which are consciously experienced as given, self-evident, are the expression of emotional needs formed in the family (essentially). The family relationships a child grows up in have a double self-sufficiency: the parent-child relationship (in which the parent quite automatically loves its own children differently from all others) is a more and more exclusive emotional bond, as other functions of the family are taken away by the state, and as a result of the changing relationships between the family and work. Secondly, the relationships within the family are given a priority over other relationships to the point where the young child often has no other relationships at all, at least not any of any emotional significance.

The child's own emotional needs are formed within this context, without his or her, or the parents' conscious knowledge of what is happening. The child, once grown, finds himself already formed with needs that he is so much living within that he can only act upon them as givens. And these needs can only be satisfied by recreating emotional relationships which have the same kind of self-sufficiency as the feelings within the family. Families are then reproduced, and the vicious circle continues.

This reproduction of the emotional needs created in the family can happen in a complicated way, so that the adult relationships are by no means the templates of the parents'. But to take the example of the different ways people have of being sexual: the differences (fancying people, wanting sex only on the basis of love), are clearly formed by the way sex is expressed in the family. For children, there is no space in the family for the expression of sex, whereas it is only in relation to parents that emotional needs are created. So, when sex does get expressed in adult life, there is an uneasy relation between sex and feelings. This uneasy relation has many variants, the two extremes are sex simply as a symbolic expression of love (as it often is in monogamous couples) and sex as completely abstracted and disconnected from any emotional relationship, as in voyeuristic, pornographic, or advertised sex.

Individualism of feelings

This first aspect of feelings, forming relationships on the basis of the given feelings such as liking and loving, means that the feelings are felt to emanate from individuals. Givenness of feelings and individuals as the original source of feelings, imply each other.

The individualism we are talking about here is not a moral concept (that people are only out for themselves, as possessive, exclusive, etc.). We are identifying a basis of relationships resulting from given feelings in which individuals are taken as the independent and ultimate source of their own action and feelings.

The individualism of personal relations is only one of the individualisms under capitalism. Individualism is a form of social relation. The individual in this sense is not to be identified with the biological entity, but is a consequence of a way of relating which constructs people as individuals. For example, the wage relation is a social relation between capital and the individual wage worker. Capitalism socialises and collectivises labour by bringing a mass of workers together through the individual wage-contract to the same capital. This individualism of the wage contract is fairly directly in contradiction to the social and mass character of the production process — it is an externally constrained individualism in at least potential conflict with the social base of production, both at the end of private individual consumption and against the private ownership of capital.

Other individualisms in capitalism are actually experienced from within, and so have different forms of contradiction, since the being an individual entity actually feels like a quality of the self, not a social relation. This is true of the individualism of personal relations, as we have argued, where feelings seem to come from oneself as a particular individual. It is also true of intellectual individualism where there is a conviction and sense that your thoughts come from your own individual process of thinking and logic and that the differences between people come from differences in their individual mental qualities and thought processes. Yet these differences between individuals are only the end product of the privatised formation within the nuclear family, and the individualised character of work in schools and universities. These individualise each one of us, concealing the social basis of the ideas we have.

So individualisms can have two aspects: the social relation that makes people into individuals, irrespective of their awareness; and the resultant subjective sense that our actions, thoughts or feelings do originate in ourselves as individuals — a sense you are not likely to have on the factory floor, but are likely to in the home or school.

Emotional individualism is the subjective sense that each individual has in forming a relationship, that each person is the source of the feelings, and that what binds the people together is each of them having their feelings for the other. This is not experienced directly as reproducing a specific form of social relation, the capitalist personal relationship. So personal relations seem to stem from each individual taken separately. Particular individual differences, effects of our past, are defended as being qualities of the unique individual. This is the basis of an individualistic sense of each person having a special identity. Relationships then seem to be a consequence of each person with a unique separate identity, making a special bond with another, and society is just made up of all these special unique bonds, separately formed. This is the characteristic subjective sense of what is in fact a general social relation. This is also why identities, the uniqueness of each separate source of feelings, have to be affirmed in personal relations to maintain this subjective sense, and why consequently when relations formed on this basis become unstuck, it is a direct threat to identity.

There are different examples of how emotional individualism plays a part in the dynamics of personal relations. It makes it possible to love or to feel sexually attracted to someone without any reciprocation at all, because there need be no other basis for a relation than having a feeling, and it is only a question of whether both do. And when love is reciprocated, the difference is just that as well as sensing the feelings coming out of oneself, one has the strong sense of the other person's feelings coming towards oneself. Part of the power of the early process of falling in love is the sense that there are two independent sources of feeling: there is a sense of the separateness and otherness of each other.

It is this sense of there being two poles that initially makes it possible for a couple to have their individual identities, as the special sources of feelings, thoughts, etc, affirmed in each other's eyes. But as the couple is established as a relationship with its own structure, there is a gradual loss of this sense of separateness which is part of the process of breakdown or boredom in love-relationships. Often only one pole, one identity, (usually the man's) survives, to be affirmed through the loss of the other person's identity. This is why, within the framework of personal relations based on individuals as sources of feelings, there is a dilemma, particularly for the woman, between dependence and independence. Too much closeness seems to destroy the 'independence' of one or both. This problem can typically be dealt with by successive changes of partner: if you lose your identity with one person, you try to find it again by falling in love with another.

So, the dependence-independence problem leads to a practice that is individualistic in the moral sense, because it arises from the emotional individualism in the theoretical sense.

The individualist dependence/independence problem is often the way Women's Liberation sees the dilemma for women. This is because it is more likely to be the woman whose feelings of separateness are submerged in the couple, because there is no other source of validation of her identity outside the love relationship. But for a man, it is often his identity constructed outside in his work that is affirmed by the woman within the couple; whereas for the woman, her identity is very fundamentally constructed by who she is for the man, inside the relationship. Therefore when she does act outside the relationship and independently of the man, this often makes her feel in conflict with her emotional life, and to feel she has the choice of either depending totally on a man, or having an independent working life without a relationship with a man.

But this choice is one forced on women only by the nature of personal relationships based on having an identity as a special unique source of feelings and thoughts. Women's experience of dependency is not a result of their individual psychological formations as dependent types; nor is the dilemma an expression of an inherent conflict between closeness/commitment and independent activity. Rather it is a contradiction which only occurs within the framework of the individualism of capitalist personal relations.

Dissociation of feelings

There is a separation, particular to capitalism, between the work and the family. This becomes a separation between the public and the private, in which emotional relationships are in dissociation from bonds other than feelings, in contrast to the feudal kinship domestic unit, for example, which was also a working unit.

Outside of work, under capitalism people's contacts with each other are often accidental collisions of people who are not involved in a common project extending beyond the relationship which would enable them to see the concrete nature of the dependence on each other. Instead, feelings are set apart as the basis of a particular type of social relationship, the personal relationship. The dynamic to set up such 'personal' relationships comes from the emotional needs created in each person by his formation in the family, not by any visible or concrete bonds between adults. The person to whom the feelings are directed doesn't even have to have the qualities for which he/she is loved: people can construct phantasy images of each other to love. This is a consequence of the setting apart of feelings to create a special type of relationship, the personal relationship.

When people meet 'socially', and form relationships on the basis of emotional needs created in the family, experienced as having feelings for each other, they can just as well spin off as collide and fuse. The original binding power of the couple in feelings is then gradually supplanted by material bonds of children, mortgages, etc., which the domestic unit elaborates. This additional 'materialisation' of the couple can then come into conflict with the evaporated basis in feelings.

The domestic unit is the institutionalised expression of the dissociation of emotional and work life, and it is within the domestic unit that women are 'concentrated'. Women therefore live their lives concretely more within one side of the capitalist fragmentation of work and emotionality, in the sphere of the exclusively private and personal, the primarily emotional. This is why the dissociation which makes feelings the basis of the personal has worse effects for women, making them specialists in the emotional.

Abstraction of feelings

There are bonds of feelings which are not abstract: for example bonds which tie workers together in a solidarity consciously based on a shared, and understood, objective situation as workers. Such feelings can be seen to be specific to the class situation of a definite social group at a definite historical period. They can be distinguished from the kinds of feelings which maintain the ruling class, such as esprit de corps, which is also the expression of a particular social situation at a particular historical moment.

An abstract feeling is a feeling which is directed towards another person as an individual apparently, or subjectively, irrespective of social context or class. While of course it is no coincidence that most personal relations are in fact between people of the same class, the subjective sense of the feelings does not seem to be one of making a class alliance, this being illustrated by the contrast sometimes made between marrying for love and not money. Love is a feeling which seems to make the relations personal as opposed to social, hence masking the social basis. It is a bond between two individuals marked off from whatever other social underpinnings there may be, and the subjective sense of those feelings is that they do have nothing to do with those social underpinnings. Love is an abstract feeling in this sense, both in the ideology of love and in the lived quality of the feelings. It is because the feeling of love is abstracted from social class or historical context, that having the feeling of love seems like a natural or human feeling to have, not a specific historical type of feeling peculiar to capitalist personal relations.

Pop songs speak of love as just love, indefinable, inexplicable, the more involuntary and mysterious the attraction the more real the love.

But in fact these feelings of love as indefinable rest on a lived reality in which the person who loves is responding to something specific in the other person. This specific aspect of the other, which is being abstracted out, is his capacity, real or imagined, to satisfy the emotional needs created in the family. If the family created the primary need to be loved as by the mother, that is the aspect of the loved one which is abstracted out and responded to in the loved one. The way this is actually experienced is through the given feelings of love.

This is why love, though it involves an abstraction from the whole complex of an individual's social situation, nevertheless tends to become a relationship that makes total demands for priority and all-inclusiveness since the family relationships which created those needs are all embracing emotional relationships.

Love displaces other real bases for relationships since it tends to become the sole basis, as it was in the family — love no matter what you do. Agreements and shared ideas become distorted by the total identification between the couple, so that eventually disagreements and differences cannot be expressed at all because they threaten the psychological identification of the couple, they threaten the abstract feelings.

Consciousness, unconsciousness and theory

The family as untheorised practice

The nuclear family emerged gradually; it was not installed as the result of conscious political practice. In this, the family is like all capitalist social relations, and the capitalist mode of production itself, which was not established as the result of a conscious political practice.

Capitalist moral and legal codes confirm the family, as it confirmed the capitalist economic relations that grew up. But the law did not create them. That is not how capitalist development occurs.

The break-up of feudal peasant agriculture created a migrant labour force, large urban centres, and made large-scale industry possible. These developments were all essential to the formation of the nuclear family. But none of these were preplanned, either as a precondition for history or for the nuclear family. But the effect was to change the whole pattern of how people formed relationships. In modern capitalism, the nuclear family is still ousting older forms as the result of developments which are not directly aimed at making this transformation: for example, the introduction of high-rise flats, or the business property development in city centres, which have been breaking down broader working class kinship patterns. A social relation which emerges in this way, not as a result of conscious political practice, is an untheorised practice.

The unconsciousness of family relationships

The family, as an untheorised practice, has the effect of making the relationships within the family unconscious. Nucleation, individualism, and all the other characteristics of feelings which we have described in the previous section, occurred without anyone trying to make them happen, so that people live these changes just at the level of effects: people only consciously experience the effects of the changes such as the feelings which subjectively seem to be the basis of personal relationships. This makes the feelings seem to stem from human nature itself, since the people didn't themselves make the structural changes that caused them to have this type of feelings.

Really, the effects are continually reproduced on the social basis that puts the family in a particular relation to production under capitalism. This doesn't mean that the effects, the feelings, are just appearances, not real. The way people experience the family only in terms of effects is the necessary mechanism for its continued reproduction — people do go on feeling feelings and forming relations on the basis of their feelings, on the basis of what are only effects. Unconsciousness of the basis of feelings has a necessary complement in a particular kind of consciousness of what is going on.

Ideology and bourgeois theory of love

The ideology of love, in law, morality, education, pop music, confirms even to the extent of parody, what actually goes on in relationships at this level of effects. Some more radical bourgeois theory, such as Freud, sees through the romantic idea of love, but refers the basis of relationships back to a psychological unconsciousness, with relationships still emanating from the individual feelings, but now just the unconscious individual feelings, repeating the relations he had in infancy to his parents. This idea of a psychological unconscious makes unconsciousness a property of each individual, and hence a natural and universal property of every single person considered separately. We think that postulating a psychological unconscious has the profoundly reactionary consequence that it cannot be seen as open to political action, unlike the idea we are putting forward in which unconsciousness is seen as a property of definite social historical relations.

Consciousness and unconsciousness of feelings

This complementary relation of consciousness which occurs in the family as a result of its not being a consciously constructed form of relationship, is also an aspect of the four different concepts explained in the first section. So, the givenness of feelings involves the conscious experience of feelings as just being given, natural, (e.g. I just do feel sexually attracted), and the unconscious aspect of their formation in the family.

Similarly, individualism has a conscious aspect, the feeling of being the independent source of one's own feelings and thoughts; and an unconscious aspect, the social relations that make us individuals irrespective of any practice of our own, and in which we are made unconscious precisely of our individualistic consciousness.

Dissociation and hence the fragmentation of life under capitalism was also not the result of a conscious project and its lived effects, such as the feelings of dependence women feel as a result of their containment within the personal, are not felt consciously to be consequences of the dissociation.

The abstractness of feelings is itself the conscious correlate of the unconsciousness of the dissociation. It isn't that people are unconscious of, or haven't noticed as a fact, the split between home and work. What they are unconscious of is the relation between some of their lived feelings and this dissociation. These examples should make it clearer how our conception of unconsciousness is a property of personal relations as a specifically capitalist and historical form of personal relations.

Structure of relationships

Personal relationships being produced at the level of effects, through the medium of abstract feelings going from one individual to another, also implies a particular structure of relationships. By the structure of relationships is meant the relationship between the couple as a sexual love relationship, and other relationships, or the relationship between personal relationships of all kinds.

The nature of individual emotionality of love creates an absolute difference between love and any other non-sexual personal relationship. All other people are related to as the 'outside'; couples relate as a unit to other people, and the greater feelings within the couple give a quite different priority to the couple over other relationships. The particular way that love and sex are combined within the couple means that sexual relations have more claims than non-sexual ones. But the character of personal relations based on feelings going from one individual source of feelings to another always creates an inside and an outside, with friendships as well as with couples — it is always a kind of contract between two people only. It is because the sexual-love relationship is accepted as having a qualitatively different claim than other relationships that this fragmentation of personal life into so many different one-to-one relationships does not always result in feelings of unease or antagonism. As long as everyone plays the game, and treats couples both as a unit and as sacrosanct, this structure of personal relations can work smoothly.

When other personal relations are sexual, though, this structure cannot continue to operate smoothly – the relationship between relationships cannot continue to be lived unconsciously, as though there were no relationship between relationships, only so many autonomous sets of feelings between two individuals. The separation of the inside and the outside of the couple is brought unavoidably into focus. Because of the total demands and the affirmation of identity that are involved in the sexual love relationship, sex with anyone else can only be tolerated if the second relationship is treated as an affair, that is, a secondary relationship, which leaves the couple intact as the basic unit. Monogamy and affairs mutually imply each other. Jealousy follows from the individualism and the abstractness of love which make it impossible for there to be a relationship between relationships other than two competing one-to-one relationships, each with their own inside and outside.

Inasmuch as the structure of relationships is based on emotional individualism with its consciousness of feelings going from one individual to another, the relationship between relationships remains unconscious, not consciously constructed, and so results in the felt effects of jealousy. The structure of relationships, therefore, also entails a particular consciousness in relation to a particular unconsciousness. So long as relationships have their basis in this type of feelings with its particular consciousness, which has a necessarily one-to-one character as the largest unit, there can be no conscious project of the construction of a relationship between different relationships, and then the real, material basis for jealousy remains.

Changing the basis of relationships

These theoretical ideas must seem pretentious and high-flown in relation to the objectively very limited nature of our practice and our life histories, out of which they have come. We can't claim to have changed the basis of our relationships when the whole basis of capitalist personal relations remains, including, most importantly, the sexism resulting from the relations of women to work and the family. Only a generalised and mass practice could change this social basis.

From our life histories we found out how each of us had wanted to change. We saw that sexism in the couple, which was felt by us variously as dependence or identification with the man, was the effect of love and monogamy; and we saw that the kinds of sexism that occur outside the couple, in the form of pornography, voyeurism, and all the forms of disconnected sex which objectify women, was the complement of monogamy. These apparently opposite manifestations of sexism, idealising and degrading women, were all effects of the same unconsciously produced relation of love and sex created in the family.

In order to get out of these patterns of relating, and to get out of the false alternatives of independence/dependence open to women, and granted that we are acting within existing conditions of capitalism, we have to think of our relationships now as a permanently on-going sexual struggle, which has somehow got to be made part of a public, political struggle.

We are trying to develop ways of relating, and don't think of what we are doing as setting up a particular structure or model of relationships (such as having two sexual relationships, or living apart as the specific contexts in which the struggle may take place). The particular structures of relationships that we have in the group are therefore not seen as an end which we have been trying to achieve as such, but as a context in which we have been trying to carry out changes in the way we relate — sexuality and emotionality, the attempt to theorise and make public our practice, the attempt to change the relation between inside and outside, to break-down the one-to-one character of relations. Although we think some of the problems we have been tackling would have to be part of any general sexual struggle under capitalism, we can only talk about them as they concretely arose for us, with our particular life histories, and the particular structures of relationships each of us is in.

For example, for the man and the woman who are now living apart, the problem has been mainly around constructing a relationship which does not become a basis from which the man can act on the outside world, but which absorbs the woman into the couple as it had done before. This is a problem common to all of us in the group. Also they have been trying to change the emotional exclusiveness that characterised their relationship while they were living together, and develop closer emotional bonds with the people they are working with. In the other relationships, involving the three other people of the group, there are other central problems involving the relationship between two sexual relationships. We can here only give some few indications of some of the ways we have tried to work out these problems.

We have tried to work out a conscious practice of constructing relationships, as opposed to the untheorised practice of pursuing the emotional dynamics of needs created within the family. One of the things this means right from the start is giving accounts to each other and to other people (in the group and outside) of what is going on in the relationship. The emotional relationships are themselves changed by being inserted into a group the basis of which is not simply to form personal relationships, but to work out a sexual politics in connection with other political activity. They are also changed by the fact that we can each intervene, with comments based on intimate knowledge, in emotional relations of which we are not part. This again changes the nature of the relationships, inasmuch as the dynamics of what goes on within a given relationship is not kept within the closed boundaries of that relationship: one-to-one emotional actions and reactions are undermined.

In the relationship involving three, the effect of this collective and public work, in which the construction of what is going on is seen as a consciously shared project, the effect has been to make sex, and the heterosexuality of the two sexual relationships, less pivotal. The structure is changed from two potentially antagonistic couples, with one person at the apex, into three people with real reasons for being together in the group, reasons other than feelings between two two's. This has the effect of actually changing the nature of the feelings felt within the two two's, from the kind of feelings that had held us in previous emotionally one-to-one relations. Once this happens, sex within one of the two sexual relations becomes less of a threat to the other. It is by trying to change things that are real and valid reasons for jealousy in relations based on one-to-one feelings, that we have been able to change the feelings of jealousy.

When there are real bonds of work and struggle among people, making the relationships also the object of common political work with people in the group who are not directly in them, the establishment of the couple as an 'inside' as opposed to the absolutely differentiated 'outside', is forestalled. This is the way in which we as women have been trying to change the basis on which dependence and over-identification can arise. If we are working together as something we have planned and understood together, we can see clearly the limits of what we can do for each other — limits which are inherent in any political practice — which prevents the kinds of emotional investment of an abstract kind, and the feeling of the total and irrational dependence women sometimes feel for men as if for an all-powerful father.

The politics of the group is about other aspects of capitalist social relations, not just sexuality and personal relations. Changes of the kind touched on above don't alter some of the major bases of personal relations, such as the dissociation between the family and work. While we may have broken down some of the divisions between what counts as personal relations and what counts as political relations, this dissociation is a structural feature of society that is not open to changes in our individual lives. When we engage in politics of housing, claimants, education, etc, we are not under the idealist illusion that by us individually being politically active in different areas we overcome their dissociation, as if to militate at home and at work is to overcome the work/family split in our own individual lives. This fragmentation is one that can only be overcome by a mass political practice in all the areas. This must be very clearly understood as a defining limitation of a sexual politics, such as we have been doing in the group.

THE FAMILY, SEXUAL POLITICS AND CAPITALISM

It's because of the very nature of capitalist personal relations (the emotional individualism, the personalisation, the abstractness from other spheres of the social formation), that a personal, sexual politics is suspected for being individualist and related only to a goal of achieving personal subjective happiness. Naturally there are also very definite reasons for being suspicious of some personal politics for exactly those reasons, of people who try, simply by changing their life-style, to create what is imagined to be a liberated enclave within capitalism.

We also have reason to be suspicious of ourselves, since what we have written is only on the basis of the minimal experience of five university-educated women and men. The particular contradictions we have felt and tried to act on, can only be variations of general ones, if they are that. The abstract emotionality of people like us may be more in relief. More, the centrality of personal relations to our lives may be greater, simply as an effect of the different relation we have to the means of production. Although some of us have, and others are going to have, working-class jobs, the space created for personal life for the rest of us (and in the past for all of us) is quite different than for the working class. The contradictions of personal life may therefore appear in a more acute form, and appear more central to people like us. If, however, we don't actually want to maintain the realm of necessity to work at the pace demanded by capitalism, it nonetheless remains that the capitalist nature of personal relations, enshrined above all in the nuclear family, is a form that pervades all classes.

Saying this, however, is only to indicate that the struggle against the family is not itself a class struggle, although articulated with it. If the family is articulated with capitalism, it is not articulated to the relation between capital and labour as such. Commodities are not produced in the family, nor is exchange value, nor is surplus value. The formation of the couple, through emotional and sexual bonds, is not itself an economic relation. To demand wages for housework is therefore to demand that the family be based on capitalist economic relations in a direct way, reinforcing the family and tying it directly to a capitalist state. Even in terms of reproducing labour-power the family does not do so on a commodity production basis. With the change in the position of the British working class in the international division of labour in imperialism, the most important centre for the reproduction of labour power has shifted outside the family to education, which also does not produce labour-power on a capitalist commodity production basis. The family concentrates on the physical reproduction of labour-power, while education reproduces the division of labour. The place of the family in this imperialist era has changed.

The family has become more and more restricted to two essential roles: as a unit for individual consumption, correlative to the individual wage labour and commodity production for individual consumption — individualised washing machinery, individualised transport, individualised homes, individualised cooking equipment, individualised (hence passive) visual stimulation (TV). Much of this obviously structures 'personal' life and it would be mistaken to view it as personal any more than other parts of the cycle of the reproduction of social capital — such as the point of production. The second essential role is that of biological reproduction, and the regulation of sexuality, which itself has, because of the dissociation of the family from all other aspects of the social formation except for individual consumption, become more and more regulated on the basis of pure sexuality — with an abstract emotionality of love to make sure that it's monogamous.

The reason and necessity for sexual politics is clear. The family is essentially reproduced through the medium of emotionality and sexuality, as well as through the patterns of individual consumption. The separation of consumption from production (which is peculiar to capitalism, where the worker no longer produces directly for his own consumption, but for the capitalist) means that a particular form of biological reproduction is combined with a particular mode of the formation of emotionality in children, which then finds expression in the reproduction of the family.

The family is not autonomous from the reproduction of capitalist social relations in general, nor is it even autonomous from the reproduction of the total social capital. But it is specific. The wage as a means of individual consumption is dissociated from the production of value at the point of production, in just the same way as the family is dissociated from the labour force at the point of production as a unit of consumption — even if the worker just travels from home to work, he is subject to different relations in the two places: at home an individual consumer, at work a collective producer. The relations of consumption are different from those of production, if connected (e.g., contradictions between individual consumption and social consumption). The relations in the reproduction of sexuality and emotionality (which we have tried to theorise above), although articulated with individual consumption, are different again.

Yet, precisely because they articulate with each other, these different relations do sustain each other. The family can act as a safety-valve for the horrors of work. Individual consumption at home can act, in its apparent dissociation from production, against taking any action at work which puts in question individual consumption — as bourgeois propaganda continually says in arguing against strikes in protection of the consumer. Similarly with H.P. commitments where payment on the never never means working for ever ever. The interpenetration of individual consumption and emotionally individualist sexual-love relations is not so far off as great as the ideological presentations of advertisements — even if the reality is not quite so crunchy.

So any political attempt to bring about a revolutionary transformation only at the point of production relies on the fact that the family is not at the same time — as the point of consumption and through emotional bonds of some power — acting as a counter-force. The revolutionary spirit will just blow these things away as the superstructural dross of capitalism? On the contrary, these forms of emotional relations are bonds, inextricably joined with individual consumption, and they act as powerful and integral forces for the maintenance of capitalist relations at the point of production. It would be a mistake to see capitalist relations of production as being established only at the point of production, and not at the point of consumption as well, when both are necessary for and integral to the reproduction of the total social capital, and to the relation between wage-labour and capital.

For example. the problem of housing cannot be dissociated from the politics of sexuality. The attempt of a recent government to introduce the laws of the market directly into the sphere of housing (*The 'Fair' Rent Act*) only emphasises what has been a recurrent and structural contradiction in consumption. Housing, paid for out of the individual wage, is submitted to the principles of normal commodity consumption and production. This suggests that wages constitute an adequate fund for a continuously expanding production of housing, on the same pattern as other commodities. But this is not so. Housing involves considerable accumulation. The fund for the expansion of housing is never met by the total social wage, constrained either to rent or to mortgage, thus entailing an endemic shortage of housing. What may be possible for the accumulation of sufficient to buy a car out of the wage, is not so possible for the purchase of the means of habitation. A relatively posh car can be found outside a slum. The problem of housing is an expression of a system which entails the purchase of housing out of the individual wage-packet competing with alternative uses of land where capital accumulation proper can take place.

To say this, however, only means that the purchaser of housing, the individual wage-labourer, has the nuclear family as its obverse, since what is purchased is the individual family housing unit, a private sphere. As a producer the worker is in a mass; as a consumer, the same person is on his own enshrined in the four walls of the capitalist housing unit, with its attempt at privatisation of all the domestic functions of cooking, washing, child-rearing. The emotional bonds of the family help hold this bit together, and shore up the four walls against intruders.

What is true of housing, the home, is true of the path from home to work. There, there is the direct conflict between the attempt to reduce transport to a commodity basis — each family with its own private means of transport; and the fact that transport as a system cannot be reduced to a commodity production basis, and has required massive state intervention to provide the necessary infrastructure. Once again this conflict results in the production of the minimum necessary infrastructure on which capitalist transport can then roam freely. But the family car is a family car, with the full ideological weight of advertisements behind it. If you challenge this system of transport, you challenge also the family as a unit with its own four wheels.

You cannot put into question the relations of production of capitalism only at the point of production, or even regard the point of the mass organisation of labour as the only basis for the power of the working class. The power of the working class to change relations of production at the point of production also depends on the willingness of the same working class to change the relations of production at the point of consumption, the family and all that holds it together. It depends on some kind of vision of what it could be to be other than four people between four walls and on four wheels, a vision based on a real wish to change all that in consequence of specific contradictions in those areas.

The family, therefore, as the point where sexual relations and relations of consumption conjoin, has its specific contradictions, ones which are not reducible to the class struggle between wage-labour and capital, but which nonetheless, depending on the balance of emotional forces sustaining or undermining the family, contribute directly to that class struggle. The contradictions articulate with each other. So must our conscious political practice. A politics which develops a practice of changing the basis of sexual-personal relations, working out the specific contradictions, as well as on their articulation with other social relations of capitalism, is therefore a necessity, even if the practice we have been talking about is tentative, uncertain, highly particular, and not at all sure of its connections with what anybody else thinks. Which is one of the reasons for writing this — to find out.

PAMPHLET TWO

INTRODUCTION

In the first pamphlet we wrote mainly about the structure of capitalist emotional relationships and the politics of changing them. Here, we develop this in two directions: first, we situate emotional relations within the family as containing economic and political relations, and in the many-sided politics of changing the family; and secondly, we write about sex and sexual relations.

But how does theory grow? In the long run, it will only develop as the struggle to change the family develops. Part of this struggle, but only a small part, will be about the ways that we, as 'middle-class militants', change ourselves. At present, though, there isn't much of a mass practice, and so we've only got our own practice to talk about when thinking about the relation between the theory and politics of the family and sexuality. This is both the reason why we have written about ourselves, and it is also the reason why there is a big leap from what we have said about ourselves to talking about the capitalist family. Writing about ourselves in a pamphlet, however, is an attempt to make our thoughts public so that a more general theory based on a more general practice can be developed. Here in this introduction, therefore, we want to write about the problems of writing theory and how it might relate to other people's experience and practice.

In the final section, we put forward a critique of Freud as an example of a theory which could never develop a revolutionary politics to replace the capitalist family. It can only theorise the existing social relations, so is both sexist and bourgeois in content. Our critique takes the form of showing that this limitation of the theory arises from the nature of psychoanalysis as the practice on which the theory rests.

Our attempts in the last pamphlet to write a theory of sexuality and sexual politics was criticised by some people for the way it related thought and feeling, the theory and the experience. People have said that the 'life histories' were too interpreted, as if we had rewritten our individual experiences and our pasts to fit our concepts. And people said the theory section was too abstract, too much a conceptual scheme without the concrete content of the experience. Both of these are valid criticisms. They point to a general political problem of the capitalist split between thought and feeling, experience: the political problem of how to change the relation between theory and experience. There can be no un-interpreted accounts of experience. But the weakness of the way we wrote that pamphlet was to have separated the life histories from the theory, as though one were a gloss on the other, or one derived from the other.

But rather than defend the last pamphlet, it would be better to talk about the problems directly. For, it isn't just a question of writing differently to overcome the split between theory and experience. It is a question of the way we are (i.e. those of us who are formed within capitalism). There is a split within us, an internal antagonism between thought and feeling, between the way we can think 'theoretically' and our everyday consciousness. In trying to write and think about sexuality here, we are very aware of this ourselves. People have a real emotional reaction against the idea of thinking theoretically about feelings and sexual attraction, as though that would magic the feelings away. This pervades a lot of sexual liberation ideas too, which glorify spontaneity above all as the mark of the truly sexual, the truly emotional experience. This is another strand of criticism we have had: theorising our sexual relationships suggests that we are supercool about sex ourselves, and are putting down people who have strong feelings, or who 'just' feel things.

These problems about writing theory are largely built up by the nature of capitalist education, in three connected ways. First, education creates a split between abstract theory and people's untheorised lived experience. This is an aspect of a split between theory and practice embodied in capitalist education. Secondly, education reproduces the hierarchical division of labour in capitalism. And thirdly, education reproduces the sexual division of labour.

The split between theory and untheorised lived experience arises from the way capitalism historically emerged: capitalist social relations and institutions emerged gradually; the way they fit together (the family with production, education with the family) was not as a result of a conscious political practice of the people as a whole. Social relations which emerge in this way are the result of an untheorised practice. In our everyday lives we live the effects of the way social relations are structured and interrelated, but we did not construct them ourselves. The other side of this is that the theory we learn in our education has a passive relation to our lived reality. Education teaches us to relate to ideas as closed systems of concepts. Above all, it does not teach theory in dynamic relation to a practice of changing reality as we live it.

It is possible to treat marxist ideas in this way too, as a system of concepts. The academic, or intellectualist, passive use of marxist concepts is to make them into given interpretative schema, a set of a priori categories like 'class', into which you just fit bits of empirical reality, really just giving new names to things that are there. This produces theory which is abstract and which reproduces existing social relations. Historically, marxism did not have this passive relation to social reality, but developed concepts in relation to an active practice to change that reality. But this connection can be systematically destroyed by a marxism that is thought in the way education teaches us to think.

The general ideas about the family which we have put forward in this pamphlet use marxist theory. The extent to which our theoretical ideas are abstract and formal is a measure of the absence of a mass political struggle to change the family. Abstractness in theory isn't a quality internal to a system of ideas itself, but depends on the actual existing social possibility for the theorisers to have an active, changing, instead of a passive, interpretative, relation to the actually untheorised reality.

Our starting point is that we have all been thoroughly conditioned by acquiring most of our knowledge and the ways we relate to thinking, through capitalist education. It is a fact peculiar to capitalism that gaining knowledge and skills takes place in a way that cuts it off from lived experience, in specialist institutions for training the mind, schools and universities. We learn to know what is in books separately from the way we know the reality to which the books may refer. 'School work', 'knowledge', sometimes felt like a special activity you 'did' at school, nothing to do with anything you saw, heard, felt or did, outside the school. In the universities, academic knowledge, especially in the social and psychological subjects, is split from what students know of their social reality, their own feelings and perceptions.

But this split between thought and experience is particularly acute in the development of sexuality, making sexuality and the emotions especially recalcitrant to being theorised and collectively constructed in a conscious political practice. For, on the one hand, there is hardly any bourgeois theory of sexuality to be put over at either school or university. (Freud was really the first, and has never been part of mainstream psychology.) The child's mind is being formed and explicitly structured by curriculum at school, while his sexuality, neither consciously formed nor explicitly structured by the school, receives little mention.

On the other hand, some of the most important of the child's emotional patterns are being formed within the family. Here, the parents' sexuality is usually not openly revealed to the child, and again sex often receives little mention. So you could almost say sexuality is formed 'undercover', because sex as such isn't allowed direct expression for the child, and is either completely submerged, or is punished if it does go on.

The process of sexual development is therefore particularly cut off, at most finding space in the crannies somewhere between the two major institutions of the child's public life, the school and the family, and is made so guilty that it can't be thought about.

This process of the formation of thought split off from the formation of sexuality, makes sexuality and emotions come to seem the very antithesis of thought. And this is how it is seen in popular ideologies (as well as some ideologies of liberated sex). But this is a political problem. For, a sexuality socially split from thought in this way, is condemned to never being open to a social and conscious attempt to change the present, passively lived, capitalist sexual relations. This means that the politics of changing the social relations of sexuality will also have to involve a politics of changing the kind of theory we write, the types of thinking and its relation to reality that we learnt in institutions of bourgeois education.

The split between theory and practice exists because the social reality of capitalism isn't constructed by a mass practice that everyone is engaged in, with everyone understanding what they are collectively constructing. This is an aspect of the class system and the division of labour, in which intellectuality is the preserve of an elite. The theory made by the intellectuals within a capitalist class system couldn't be related to a mass practice to change that system. Capitalist education, through successive examinations and selection, is the instrument which reproduces these divisions among people in the way they relate to thinking and knowing, to theory, and even to reading anything at all. Education helps to reproduce both a hierarchical and a sexual division of labour.

First of all, the hierarchical division of labour. Education channels people into different levels of the labour force, from the mental workers at the top to the manual workers at the bottom, with various layers of skill and expertise in between. Anyone who writes anything theoretical at the moment is therefore likely to be university educated. The examination system not only cuts off 80 per cent of the population from higher education, but also creates elites within elites, within and between universities, polys, etc. Because writing theory goes so much with passing and failing examinations, theory as such is intimidating, since it is a provocative mark of the division between the educational 'successes' and 'failures'.

Some people felt this about our last pamphlet: it was intimidating by being too heavy and theoretical. This is an aspect of the general political problem about theory, which is really a problem about the social relations of knowledge created by the division of labour. There aren't any individual and short term solutions to this, like writing differently, or not trying to work out any theory at all. These are problems that can only be tackled in the long term by transforming the educational system itself. In the meantime, of course, this doesn't mean that we as educated individuals in revolutionary politics should just accept the way we have been formed to think, nor only write theoretical things. We should try to work out theory, and then present it, in a way that does not reproduce the capitalist split between theory and lived experience, as much of the standard format revolutionary writing does. More generally, though, it means that the development of a political theory and practice of any aspect of society, including sexuality and the family, must be linked with developing a politics of education, a political struggle inside education against its hierarchical nature, academicism, and competitive individualism.

Equally, there needs to be a political struggle against the sexual division of labour which the education system reproduces, interlocked with the hierarchical division of labour. Theory couldn't be related to the lived relations of the family because the sexual division of labour reproduces a specific relation between theory and the emotions. Men are formed for the labour market, and education produces in them a scientific and bureaucratic rationality at the higher levels of the labour force, a technical-practical mentality at the point of production. Women's education on the whole prepares them for the domestic roles, or for the dual roles of housewife and worker. As workers on the labour market women generally perform service and routine work at the lower levels of the female labour force, and social types of job in the professions that employ most women — teaching, nursing, social work. In reproducing women's position in the division of labour, education fosters the qualities suitable for their dual caring and serving roles inside and outside the home — artistic, domestic, literary subjects, rather than scientific and practical; nurturing the intuitive rather than the logical, the emotional rather than the technical.

This produces the deformations of male theory: its impersonality, its abstractness, making knowledge and reason instruments of male control; and it produces the anti-theoretical sensibility of women, disarming resistance through limiting it to emotional reactivity. Men are split in one way: to suppress emotions and to develop knowledge and skills which bear no relation to themselves. Women specialise in the emotions, and combine this with their anti-theoretical formation, so that emotionality as such becomes anti-theoretical.

So a theory about sexuality will only be able to develop in relation to a mass practice changing these relations to theory which are built into the capitalist hierarchical and sexual division of labour. Where we who are writing this pamphlet have started from is conditioned by our own place in this division of labour, and by our own attempts to change the split between experience and an academic relation to theory — which doesn't necessarily mean becoming less theoretical. What we've just been saying about the sexual division of labour implies that there is simply one education for men and another for women.

But this is to oversimplify. The educational system does give a minority of women the possibility of acquiring a characteristically deformed male relation to abstract theory. This is perhaps particularly true in those subject areas, notably the social and psychological sciences, where male and female positions in the division of labour are more undifferentiated. Maybe there is a trend to there being more and more such women in other fields, if their skills are needed in an expanding economy. In many other respects than in their formal education, highly educated women like this will have been formed with a specifically feminine consciousness. This produces a direct contradiction often felt by them, not present when a woman's education and her female situation coincide. This is true for the women who were involved in writing this pamphlet. We've tried to show, in accounts of ourselves, how these contradictions have interacted with our sexual relations, and how this is different for men.

The point is that because of our past education there are limits to the generality of the theory in the pamphlet, and to the generality of our practice. There are two major limitations. First, our theory can only be addressed to those who have had a formation like our own, and it is also most likely that only this small minority will have any empathy with our experience. We cannot write except in a formal way about working class families, because we aren't working class, and we haven't been engaged with working class people in a political struggle around the family — there isn't any. We could only begin to partially overcome this limitation by trying to work politically alongside the working class, in jobs or in working class organisations like tenants' associations.

Secondly, within this specific class position, we are a small group, with a limited experience and practice. We could not write anything about a number of absolutely central areas in the politics of sexuality and the family; and must rely on others to do so. Most important, we have not been able to write anything about children, as none of us has any. Nor have we written about homosexuality. This is not to give any privilege to heterosexual relationships, so much as to say that we in particular can write meaningfully only about them. Also in writing about how we've tried to change our sexual relationships, we don't want to imply that to engage in sexual politics you have to be in a sexual relationship. We think that the political struggle is to create general social conditions under which sexual relations are possible — against the prevailing conditions of sexism and capitalism — and this can be made as much by people who don't happen to be, or who don't choose to be, in a sexual relationship, as by others who are.

So for all these reasons, we want to emphasise that although we have put forward some beginnings of a theory of the capitalist family, this is a bit top heavy, because its basis in practice is so limited. Consequently much of the theory remains formal and partial. This could only change with the development of a more general political practice.

This pamphlet has been written by three of us in the group. For the purpose of the pamphlet, we call ourselves Anne, Mary, and Pete. While much of what is written has been informed by the experiences of the whole group, this pamphlet concentrates on our own. Again, this is not to give any privilege to the particular structure of relationships involved, but expresses what we in particular can write about.

POLITICS
AGAINST THE FAMILY

Later we shall be dealing more closely with sex and sexual relations as such. But here, we will be concerned with the relation between different types of social relations, sexual, political, economic, as they occur within the family, and also about the way they are known. We will do this from two perspectives: how these relations have been for us, and how we've tried to change them; how they are for the capitalist family, and what kind of political strategy against the family is necessary to deal with the complicated reality of the capitalist family. No struggle against capitalist sexual relations or the family can be seen either as 'subjective' or as concerning only sexuality.

These two perspectives do hang together: the way we look at ourselves and have tried to change affects the way we have analysed the capitalist family. Conversely, if we could not understand what we were doing in the context of its general social implications, we might just as well forget about it as politics. There is a question as to what relevance our practice, (the practice of middle class, university educated people who do not start from the reality of parents in a nuclear family) has for a general struggle against the family. It's all very well to say that our practice has affected our theory of the capitalist family. But maybe it has affected in just such a way as to make it a totally useless theory for developing a general political struggle, due to our own class position.

There's no easy answer to this question. To the extent that the theoretical thoughts we're putting forward have a basis in a very limited practice, the analysis of the capitalist family is bound to be formal, and external. But that is just a statement about how, at present, there is in fact no general working class struggle against the family. The split between the 'subjective' and 'objective', between the two perspectives, only reflects the present real limitations of our practice as a practice of a few individuals, which appears subjective only because it is an account of only us, and has not the 'objective' reality of a mass social practice.

The relation between the two perspectives is such that you can read the pamphlet in two ways. Either you can now turn to p69 and see how the relation between economics, politics, sex and knowledge has been for us and then come back to p59 to see how that has affected the way we have analysed the family. Or you can go straight ahead, and see the account of the capitalist family as being an account of the general social context, as we understand it, which defines our practice too, as a rather particular sub-species.

THE CAPITALIST FAMILY

In the first pamphlet, we talked of there being a dissociation between the family, as the centre of our emotional formation, and production, a dissociation between the family and the factory. This, we argued, was a result of the historical separation of production from consumption peculiar to the capitalist economy.

Here, in this pamphlet, we want to put forward the idea of a much more fundamental kind of dissociation, one which occurs between different social relations, (economic, political, sexual) even when they are found together in the same institution, such as the family. There is not only a dissociation between institutions, the factory and the family; there is also a dissociation which occurs within the family between the economic, sexual and political relations that are present there. To talk about dissociation between these relations even when they are found together, even when they are systematically found together, means thinking of dissociation in a deeper sense than a straightforward, 'visible', dissociation between institutions. Economically the family is at once the unit for the consumption of commodities produced under capitalist conditions of production, and a domestic economy where the labour of women is spent in a way typical only of capitalist economies although not in itself commodity production. As such it contributes to the reproduction of labour power, and the physical reproduction of children. Sexually and emotionally, the monogamous heterosexual couple is the most general form of sexual relation, and the family acts both to maintain that and reproduces the emotional needs and sexuality in children which find expression in adulthood in the reproduction of the family. Politically, the family is the home of the individual voter in the capitalist political relations of parliamentary democracy.

All these social relations of capitalism are found together within the family. But what is the relation between them? In looking at the relation between economic and sexual relations, between political and sexual relations, we will argue that what characterises the relation between these different social relations is that, although they are systematically found together as a result of the historical development of the family, there is no systematic principle that governs the way they interact with each other, so that they form no coherent system. Rather they coincide, each with its own principles, its own coherencies and contradictions, which mean that when they do interact, it has the effect of 'interference'.

Just to give one illustration of this, a woman may begin an emotional relationship, the dynamics of which may lead to a marriage 'for love'. As a consequence, the woman may become dependent on a man's wage, and her work in the domestic economy will put her into a relation to men, which although it might reinforce any emotional submissiveness, is nonetheless a specifically economic form of oppression, stemming from the general character of capitalist economic production. But the dynamics of love and economics need not continue to reinforce each other; the love can come and go, while the economic constraints of the domestic economy can remain. The point is that the primary dynamic of love is not to set up a particular form of domestic labour, or to create a unit of consumption.

The laws of capitalist economics, the wage-commodity relations, can determine the proportion of women's labour that goes on inside the domestic economy, and the proportion that is socialised and goes on outside (e.g., laundries can turn washing into a commodity service paid for out of the wage, where previously it was a domestic service carried out by women inside the home). But the systematic laws of economics have a quite specific principle which is not coherently articulated with the dynamics of emotional relations: the degree of domestic economic service determined by the development of capitalist production does not go with the degree of emotional love. There are no common principles which embrace the economic, political, and sexual social relations of capitalism.

Instead, they coincide within the family, each with its own specific principle of determination. This does not mean that they don't interact with each other, even in systematic ways. For example, the domestic unit, the mortgage and children can constrain people to go on relating to each other emotionally in ways far removed from the blissful harmonies of love. But there is no coherent overall structure. It is this relation between relations, even within the same institution, that is dissociation in a more fundamental sense. This, we shall argue later, is directly a consequence of the nature of development of capitalism, where there is no conscious political practice constructing what relation there is between sexual, economic and political social relations. The importance of discussing what the relation between the different relations is within the capitalist family, is that there can be no global smash-the-family politics, but different forms of struggle against the different relations as they coincide within the family, with their own internal contradictions as well as with contradictions between them. And also some attempt to think through what relation between these relations any political practice is trying to construct.

Economics and sexuality

Here we are dealing with the relation between economic and sexual relations. We don't go into a political economy of what those economic relations are in any depth, but hope to in the future.

Because capitalism imposes a separation between the sphere of commodity production and the sphere of consumption and the domestic economy, economic relations coincide with emotional ones in a very particular way within the family. The economic individualism of the wage contract finds its most acute expression in consumption, not in production, and as such reinforces the other basis of the domestic unit, the emotional individualism on which the personal relationship is based.

This has particular significance for domestic labour, women's work. For, in separating a sphere of the domestic economy from commodity production, the family becomes a place where purely private labour takes place. This labour is less socialised even than in pre-capitalist economies. This is because, as commodity production socialised some labour, at the same time it de-socialised and individualised commodity consumption (paid for out of the individual wage); and much domestic labour consists in expending further labour on those commodities (washing, cleaning, cooking, etc.), but in the home.

But because this labour coincides with the emotional relationship, the emotional bond is inextricably connected with the woman's economic service. Work becomes infused with the emotional nexus of the family. Refusing to work would be like going on emotional strike. Because of the primacy of the emotional basis in initiating the personal relationship, the woman's work can be experienced as so much a labour of love as not to be labour at all, just a form of caring. What is in fact a general social form of the daily replacement of labour power of the man, or in the case of children, the reproduction of the human forces of production, can, because of the 'emotional origin' of the family, appear as an expression of emotions, a sacrifice. And, this is only seen as a relation to one's own particular man/children, as a consequence of having feelings for them. In fact it is not the feelings that particular individuals have for particular individuals that are the origin of the general form of the domestic economy, within the capitalist mode of production. The fact that they may appear so is only a consequence of the way in which the domestic economy is found together with emotional relationships within the family, rather than having been consciously articulated with each other. People do not set up a domestic economy in order to fall in love. Nor are the emotional bonds which initiate and sustain personal relations experienced as having an inner aim to set up a domestic economy as an adjunct necessary to commodity production.

Of course, this assumes that the way that emotional and economic individualism coincides within the family is always non-contradictory. But because economic and sexual relations are co-present within the family only in an empirical way, and not as a result of conscious combination, they can each follow their own dynamic and become contradictory to one another. Women's economic bondage or dependence on a man's wage can be resented, and so lead to particular forms of struggle, say for the social-isation of the domestic economy, or the economic independence of women, which will undermine the mystification of women's work being a form of emotional sacrifice, an index of her love.

Conversely, the emotional dynamics of the couple entail contra-dictions which we discussed in the first pamphlet. The nature of this dynamic can lead to attempts to change sexual partners, or more funda-mentally the nature of sexual deviations. In either case, the emotional contradictions can come up against the constraints of the domestic economy, particularly in relation to bringing up children. The inner dynamics of the emotional relation however take place with no necessary connection to the whole framework of the domestic economy within which they occur, and which may force people to go on relating emotionally even when, of itself, the emotional relation would have ended.

This only demonstrates that any political struggle in the sphere of sexuality and emotionality, cannot ignore what the relations are between sexual relations and the domestic economy. You can't change one without this having implications for the other, and any politics of the family must begin to work out alternatives, at a general social level, to the capitalist dissociation between economic and sexual relations.

Politics and sexuality

In talking of politics here, we mean that there are specific social forms of political relations for the capitalist state. Our political struggle is to change capitalist political relations. Here we want just to look at two aspects of the social form of political relations as they concern the family: the political individualism which goes with elections — not the five yearly exercise of power by the people, but the five yearly resignation of collective power to individualised voting; and secondly, the fact that the political power of the capitalist state defines some areas as political — e.g. the minor adjustments made to the capitalist economy — and excludes others from the domain of politics, such as the family. The nature of the political relations defines what kinds of powers the capitalist state has, and therefore what kind of areas can be touched by its politics: the rest is left to 'consumer choice', 'private life', or 'nature'.

The individualisation of politics through voting — where the only collective aspect is the mere arithmetical adding up of all the votes cast individually — is directly complemented by the family and emotional individualism. At work, the working class does exercise some collective power, at least potentially antagonistic to political individualism. But the family is the residence of the individual voter, where individual consumer choice and individual political choice, and individual emotional choice coincide. The family is itself not only excluded from being an area of political intervention by parliament (laws on divorce, abortion, inheritance etc, only confirm its existence), but is directly depoliticising: it separates an area of emotional security from the world outside. That split, between the emotional base and the public world is absolutely integral to the political relations of capitalism. As the place where people live as individuals separate from their collective social existence, it is absolutely crucial to the maintenance of the capitalist parliamentary state.

What this means is that any politics of sexuality has not only to change sexual relations, but also the relation between sexual relations and political relations. A struggle against the family is a struggle against the social forms of the capitalist state. It is an attempt to change the whole basis in the family of political individualism, through the formation of collective power. This is crucial. For, male politics has avoided this issue. Male working class politics at the point of production leaves unscathed, indeed often reinforces, the basis of political individualism in the home, for example in fighting for greater private consumption. This is not to deny at all the importance of working class struggle in the factory, merely to indicate that it will be limited provided it is limited to the factory. For, so long as collective power is exercised only at work, it can rest at peace with the parliamentary regime which carries on quietly at home. Each time parliament tries to resolve the class struggle through the ballot box, it shifts, often successfully, the locus of politics from the factory to the individual in the family.

That is the importance of developing a collective power for challenging the family. As it is, the family is an effective counterweight to working class power. And it would be quite wrong to assume that because the woman is more in the home she is made more politically backward, simply on the mechanical grounds that she is more in it.

For a man, politics at work and emotional security at home can operate in a complementary way. And if this is so for the man, this fundamentally limits the struggle at the factory to such things as wage claims which presuppose family commodity consumption. This is not so for women. Women organising collectively already challenges their politico-emotional subordination in the family and to the family man, and ultimately the privatisation and depoliticisation of the family. The point isn't to politicise the family. The political solidarity between women creates a new political unit challenging the one-to-one relation that each woman has to a man in the family, and hence the family itself. This challenges the dissociation in the relation between the sexual and political relations of the capitalist social formation. It means struggling for different kinds of working class collective power than those that leave the family be.

Knowledge relations and the family

As we've argued, the dissociation between the different social relations as they coincide within the family, is only one side to the same coin of which the other is the fact that those social relations were not consciously constructed in a collective political way by the people who live them. The existence of the family as an individualising, de-collectivising unit show that. In the last pamphlet, we pointed out how the family, as the centre of consumption and emotions separate from production, emerged in an untheorised way. Because of its privatisation, which means that people aren't continually having to account either to themselves or to others for their private lives, the family, and the emotions that sustain it, are particularly resistent to being thought about let alone theorised. (Unlike the social form of sexual relations in primitive societies, where people can not only account to the anthropologist for their sexual relations, but also theorise it.)

Because of the untheorised way in which the different social relations coincide within the family, those relations are experienced only at the level of effects: whereas the particular form of love peculiar to the capitalist nuclear family is a consequence of the division between the family and production, and the dissociation between the different social relations: we don't, while we live within those structures, directly experience this social basis of love. We just feel, and just experience those feelings as coming from within us as individuals, not as a general social phenomenon at all.

More, in terms of the dissociation between the different relations, each of the relations has its own relation between the way it is consciously experienced and its unconscious basis. Thus the economic wage-commodity relation or wage-capital relation is such that there is no direct experience of the basis on which money changes hands, or buys commodities. But this unconsciousness, which is a structural aspect of economic relations under capitalism and of the way that they are experienced, is quite specific to economic relations. As economic relations, they are not experienced as having their origin within the individual, and indeed can be experienced directly as a social constraint (e.g. the experience of poverty on low wages). With emotional relations, however, the fact of experiencing them directly obscures, and makes unconscious, their social nature, since personal relations are felt to be a consequence of the feelings coming from within the individual, and not as the general social form of capitalist sexual relations.

Each type of social relation carries its conscious and unconscious aspect, presents a specific experience and has an underlying structure, which, because not produced by theorised political practice, is unconscious. This is a structural aspect of the different social relations, inherent in them. We think that this is one of the basic reasons for rejecting any psychological notion of the unconscious, where each individual is supposed to have a conscious or unconscious part of his mind, as if the unconsciousness were a property of the mind and not of the social relations we live.

Dissociation between the different social relations within the family means, therefore, that each individual has a fragmented consciousness, a consciousness and unconsciousness of economic relations, a consciousness (and unconsciousness) of emotional relations, and so on: but no integrated consciousness. To have an integrated consciousness implies having an integrated collective practice, in which the different social relations are consciously and politically put into relation to each other in an integrated overall structure. This is precisely what capitalism, and the nature of its historical development, prevents.

This only emphasises the fact that the point where we start from, as each individual, is having a fragmented consciousness. The only way to develop an integral theory is through developing a collective and articulated practice against the different relations which now, in a dissociated way, underpin the family. In this respect it's perhaps worth commenting on a general confusion in the left groups when they define the area of sexual politics as subjective, as opposed say to the economic oppression of women. Even if there is a discrepancy between the 'subjective' experience of economic relations and their underlying structure (of which marxism is the theory), this isn't seen as an insurmountable obstacle to a political transformation of the relations of production.

It is only in the realm of the emotions and the family that some left groups interpret the subjective experience of individuals as meaning that emotional life is, in and of itself, subjective. They make the private and individual equally subjective, and emotions no more than a subjective experience. Each time they do this, so dismissing the politics of sexuality and many of the most important aspects of the women's movement, they merely demonstrate the extent to which they have been taken in by the bourgeois separation of private and public life (which in any case is often directly reinforced by their own practice and functioning as political groups). The struggle against sexism, against the social relations of sexuality and emotionality, and the other social relations with which they coincide in the family, is no more subjective than the struggle against economic relations outside the family.

Forms of political organisation

Here we are posing some problems about organisation that arise from the analysis of the family as comprising different dissociated relations. We aren't able to suggest organisational forms. There is not very much concrete politics of the family which would be the practical basis for thinking properly about organisation. But there are some political implications about organisation that we would like to raise for discussion.

First, because the family contains the different social relations of economics, sexuality, and so on, any 'smash the family' mentality is simplistic. A political struggle around the family will have to be many-sided. Contradictions exist between the different social relations, and this means that any politics has to consciously combine the struggle against the different relations. This raises questions of organisation, because the different relations involve different kinds of practice. To struggle against individual family housing, or against the domestic economy, for example, entails some kind of mass practice, in tenants' associations or campaigns in the women's movement. On the other hand the struggle around capitalist emotions and sexuality, since it is practically related to the particular personal relations of all the individual people, and needs a fairly intensive personal knowledge of each other, seems to need a small group type organisation. So the political task of a politics of the family would have to find ways of articulating these different kinds of groupings in order to articulate the different aspects of the struggle.

Second, though, there are political implications arising from the analysis of the importance of the family in maintaining the capitalist relations of production as a whole. The political issues of the family have to be raised in other areas of politics: housing, education, and the industrial struggle. This has the organisational implication that there needs to be provision for the small group type of ongoing meeting necessary to explore family and personal politics in these other areas too. At present, there is a lot of political activity in these different areas, but they are mainly fragmented from each other, as well as from a politics of the family. This drastically limits the impact in their separate areas; if the fight in industry for collective action ignores the workers' existence outside the factory as a tenant, then the individual worker's material dependence on an individual house paid for with his wage, will continue to reinforce the bondage of workers to the wage system. When housing, school or other politics carry on in the absence of any politics of the family, the demands can assume and even shore up the family: the demand for increased community participation in schools can in practice mean increased parent involvement. If pursued uncritically, in the context of most existing schools, this means bringing together the two authorities over kids, leaving them no loopholes at all.

At the moment, the political activities that are going on which are connected with the family, are also fairly disconnected from each other. These include the nursery campaigns, the fight for equal pay, the abortion and contraception campaigns, claimants' demands for unsupported mothers against the cohabitation rule, work at women's centres, the practices of radical feminists and gay women, consciousness raising, and so on. The women's movement is just beginning to work out the ways in which the personal moves-forward that we make in consciousness raising groups, say, can be integrated with the attempts to develop a theory of the family, and with the practical campaigns which take place in more public organisational forms. There has been a split in the movement between the private and the public, though that was always the opposite of the intention; this has a distorting effect on the kind of politics of the family that is possible, with a big divide between the campaign and the consciousness raising group.

So the political tasks for a politics of the family are to begin to find organisational forms to link the different aspects of the struggle; and to provide for different ways of meeting together and organising appropriately to different dimensions of the struggle. On the first point, this isn't a question, obviously, of individuals or small groups of militants such as the group we are in, trying to take part in and integrate all the aspects of their own practice, but of building links between the different kinds of groupings with their different kinds of activity. It's a question at present of the comrades and sisters in the different areas making links, theoretical and practical.

Small groups working around sexual politics should not be opposed to mass organisation, as if they signified subjectivity and a retreat from politics. If it is in the context of wider political activity, the small group should be part of mass organisation. The aim shouldn't be to make all small meetings bigger on the road to politicisation, but to generalise the practice of sexual politics taking place partly in small groups. At present there is a big problem about this. If it is not in the context of other political work and activity around the family and other political areas, 'sexual politics' can step in to fill the vacuum, and can be dissociated from other aspects of politics, as sexuality is from other aspects of capitalist reality. The small group can then become the base group, instead of one partial form of organisation. Then the group can become an emotional centre opposed to the alien outside, serving the same kinds of functions that capitalist personal relations already do; and it becomes that much harder to work politically with other people. The problem, which we have found in our group, is how to build up our own practice in a way that does not dissociate a politics of sexuality from struggles against capitalist economic, political, and knowledge relations.

POLITICS OF
OUR OWN SEXUAL RELATIONSHIPS
Contradictions in past relationships

What we have to say about ourselves is mainly about our personal and political relationships, not about the family as defined in the previous sections. So the contradictions we experienced will be different in content from those of the family, particularly the working class family. As children we were all brought up in professional middle class families. As adults now we have no children of our own, and the women do not depend on a man for economic support. We haven't faced contradictions between parliamentary, or anti-parliamentary/revolutionary politics, and our 'personal lives'.

In the individual accounts for each of us which follow, we have tried to trace the way the sexual-emotional and political bases of the couple relationships we were in became contradictory. Although these contradictions just wouldn't occur in most families, it was in thinking about how we had come to such insoluble impasses in our own sexual relationships that we came to think afresh about what kind of theory could be developed for the family.

Mary

"I was in a couple based on love, and we wanted to work together as comrades. But what went on between us emotionally swamped what should have been the different dynamics of a working political relationship. It ended up with neither of us being able to work with each other, and with me feeling that my identity as 'political' had got so tied up with my feelings for him that I couldn't know how to begin to work politically with other people on a political rather than just purely personal basis. This was partly because a lot of what I had learned in the years that we were together had been political ideas, not enough practical work with others, so that it was the way my ways of thinking had got entangled with, and disconnected from, my ways of feeling that was contradictory. What I'm going to tell here is how feeling and thinking were put into a relationship in my own family, and how the kind of couple we were, reproduced the conditions for this in a particularly acute way.

In my family, I was loved unconditionally by my parents; they gave as much love and attention, it seemed, to us two children as to each other; we did a lot of things together, shared most things, there weren't private rooms or cupboards, or anything. My father was very much present and involved with the family, especially me. I can remember no single occasion when my parents quarrelled with each other or even seemed irritable or cross with each other. So I rarely had cause to feel excluded or rejected or cut off from the people I loved.

This meant I had an unreflective, absorbed kind of relationship with my parents and to my brother. Nothing happened to make me distance myself from them, or separate myself off with any sense of having an identity that was different from them, or 'other'. This was as true with my father as with my mother: I was brought up with the idea that I would lead an active life outside the home, and have a job. Marriage wasn't held up as my main aim, (though it was assumed that I would get married). I think my father identified with me too, hoping that I would be what he would have liked to be like.

So as a child I can remember no sense of an inner private self, as distinct from me as I related to other people. I didn't make judgements about other people, or think things out about them or myself. I was amazed for a long time when I first went to university and met more people, when it dawned on me that people had 'theories' about each other, and looked behind how other people acted and appeared. I just related to people in a very 'within' them kind of way, or didn't relate to them. I read a lot of novels and plays, and I related to people in them in the same way. I didn't ponder about them: I identified with them, and took them as models, treating literature as a kind of extension of life, a social documentary, not an art.

I would talk a lot with my parents and brother (though I was painfully shy and horribly polite with anyone else), speaking out my feelings, observations, stories, enactments in a kind of continual running commentary; so the 'me', what 'I' was, was very much a relationship with them. All my games, work and achievements, were directed towards them, not done in any sense for myself, for perfectionism, or an intrinsic goal. This didn't mean I wasn't absorbed in activities for their own sake: the more any activity was involved with the person I loved, the more it was to be intrinsically absorbing for me. I didn't do things for their praise exactly; they didn't praise me directly nor treat me as a performing child at all. It is more true to say that in doing other things, this was part of the relationship to them. On rare occasions when I was naughty and upset them, I always apologised immediately afterwards, to heal the separation as fast as possible. Once when I was about eight, I sent them a rather sentimental note through the window saying sorry, I love you, etc. I never sulked. I never ever sulked even once. It has always been too great a risk.

But mostly I wasn't naughty, and I hardly ever failed at the things I did, so I never had to confront or reflect on the relation between the love relationships and other activities I did in the outside world. I didn't meet many other adults, who would have been a jolt to my framework, and from the age of five till ten I had one very close girl friend who practically lived with us most of the time, and I was reticent with other kids, except a few neighbours and a couple of cousins. Where there is no resistance or shock to the normal way things interact, you never have a way of seeing what the connections are. Consciousness comes from conflict and contradictions being felt. I went through childhood and adolescence with an unconscious and intimate entwinement between my emotional attachments to people, and my emotional involvements with other projects and ideas.

I grew up into someone who was very much more able to have a close, exclusive all-involving personal relationship with one person, than any other kind of relationship; and much more able to express myself in a speaking dialogue, a free-wheeling thinking-aloud kind of interaction, with one person, than able to contain and elaborate thoughts and reflections inside me and in private. I used to feel I only thought when I was speaking with another person I was emotionally close to; the rest of the time I would either be using the top half of my brain to do my school or university work, or else I would dream. I think now that my aim in thinking and telling people what I thought outside school and university contexts, was primarily to make myself transparent to the other person, as though speech could weave a web of emotion and meaning between two people that made them not separate, and completely accessible to each other. This kind of illusion does sometimes happen, and can seem to be a basis for a many-sided emotional and intellectual and political commitment to each other.

These characteristics I grew up with meant that well into my twenties personal relationships that weren't one-to-one, (that is, groups of friends), or relationships not based on complete loving identification, and relationships for reasons other than emotional involvement, were always pale and formal, and were really outside my capability: I couldn't feel how they emotionally worked at all. Thinking and loving, reflecting and interacting, were split at one level, entangled at another. I was 'good' at school and university work, but it was more like cleverly applying or criticising intellectual rules of more or less complexity, than really thinking out anything for myself. I functioned completely differently when it came to trying to think about something I was serious about and had a real commitment to, like 'literature' and the 'starving Third World' in my teens, and then revolutionary politics. Then my thoughts were always in the context of being addressed to the loved person who shared my commitments, and were blocked by my feeling panicked by his judgements or overawed by his eloquence. There was also something about the way I had always expressed myself directly to my parents that had got linked up with what it meant to me to love: I found it very hard not to just try and use my thoughts and ideas as part of the relationship, mainly, rather than for the extrinsic aims they were about, like politics. But I also had a very ambivalent attitude towards sitting down and trying to write out anything of length, that would have needed a lot of private thinking before anyone else would have access to it: I would oscillate between wishing I could, but not being able to, and then furiously concealing anything I had written or thought on my own, in a really compulsive way, as if I had done something wrong, or something I was ashamed of. I have heaps of notes I've never dared look at again myself, let alone give to anyone else to read.

So I only thought out anything properly in short, discontinuous bursts that were patterned by my emotional relationships. Anything that I have written here is probably still partly directed towards pleasing or justifying myself to, or getting the approval of, various people I've loved. It's so deep rooted, that it will be ages before I can stop doing it, if ever.

I am not saying that the solution would simply have been to do private, independent, work of my own — to be more effective as a bourgeois individual. The point is that because political relations became identified for me with the interactions in the couple, the kinds of emotional absorption I described, this made it difficult to form political relations and work out political problems with people I didn't emotionally identify with, and who therefore posed obstacles I would have to struggle with to relate to them.

The couple I was in unwittingly reproduced rather pure conditions for eliciting the structure of relations between thought and feeling, and hence the political and emotional bases of the relationship, that I had derived from my family. This was precisely because we were a 'political couple'. This meant that all our activities were together, in the context of the love relationship; there was a continuous dialogue; we hadn't the usual split between home and work of the normal professional couple, which would have continued the alienated split which I had experienced at university. This alienated split was what we were trying to overcome. This gave an added sharpness to the contradictions between the different bases of the relationship. We tried to bring into association two bases of the relationship (working together; love and sex) which are normally dissociated, but which had been put into a relation to each other in the past in an emotional structure like our present one. We were not aware of the connections, we had no conscious way of relating the two within the present relationship. We tried to fuse them by a political and ideal view that it should be so. This was contradictory because of the way the relations are unconsciously entangled.

I have come to think that the 'political couple' with a special political partnership coterminous with a sexual love relationship, is contradictory. It seemed at the time to be a progressive thing to be doing, insisting on an equality between the man and the woman united by a serious mutual aim and work; and it was a profounder basis of personal solidarity than just romantic feelings. But in fact the couple based on individual sexual love reproduced patterns of feeling that distort a political relationship by placing it on too special a footing that is non-sensical for a political relationship.

This was why we have now come to the idea of consciously constructing the way sexual and political relations combine in an emotional-sexual relationship: not to split them in a capitalist way, nor to fuse them just by wishing, so that they are each others' undoing. What we actually tried concretely to do was initially guided by what we thought was going on in these past relationships."

Pete

"In a love-marriage situation, I was involved in a number of contradictions between what I was wanting out of a personal relationship and what I might be trying to do politically: I did not look at the personal relationship itself politically, and indeed used it as a kind of emotional base from which I might act politically. But this contradiction was masked for a long time, since in effect, I simply thought politically, did theoretical work, and was only peripherally involved in student actions which I disdained to a certain extent, with a combination of marxist intellectual purism and using intellectual work as a defence against coming to terms with any people outside my personal relationship. I could have what I *thought* affirmed within my personal relationship — I was the male ego-thinker, the one that did theory, without having to think too much about any contact that that thought might have with an external reality.

But this changed, and with it the relationship between being political and personal changed. So long as I was a fairly classical type of marxist intellectual on the road to becoming a marxist academic, some-body who could just treat marxist concepts as a body of truth, and remain passive towards those ideas in the same way as any bourgeois sociologist, the marriage situation was perfectly concordant: loved as the contemplative thinker, as the individual, and as the male 'I think'. The whole thing could be contained within the personal relationship. There was a dissociation between the political and the personal, since my work was one thing, our relationship another. But at the same time, the dissociation did not become an active contradiction while the 'politics' were just ideas.

In becoming involved politically in actions with other people, this immediately put this dissociation in active contradiction. This was because as the centre of my life, the relationship had incorporated everything to an extreme degree, and so was threatened when political activity meant practical involvement with other people. What I was doing politically was coming into conflict with my own emotional needs for a love relationship. It also meant a direct conflict with my wife's position in the couple. Either the political involvement could also become us as a couple unit. This seemed fraught with the contradictions that she would be political with me, not on clear political grounds, but on the grounds of the emotional relationship. Or it would mean each of us, or one of us, individually acting politically independently of the couple, in which case political ties would come into conflict with emotional ones, with a whole range of idiotically false problems over which was more important, love or politics. The choice of either alternative led to impossible contradictions between political activity and living within the couple.

This problem was also founded in the intrinsic sexism of the love relationship, in which I was being affirmed as the person who loved, thought, had a serious aim in life, as an individual, whereas my wife's identity was progressively undermined inside the relationship on the political level, as the one who got all the ideas from me.

But there is no sense me being affirmed as an individual source of thoughts and feelings, if the political aim is to construct a collective way of developing thought in relation to action. I had to get out of being the kind of individual I had been, and this meant getting out of a relationship based on the mutual affirmation of individuals as the sources of thoughts and feelings. Of course, at the time it didn't appear like this: at the time it was a succession of confused tensions, arguments, scenes, when I was quite within, and couldn't get out of, arguments of the love versus politics variety. I also think that the particular form of love relationship which I had, with its origins for me in a family that had also tried to be a completely self-sufficient world of its own, exacerbated the contradictions between individual love and collective political practice to breaking point, and made the dissociation between being political and having personal relationships particularly acute."

Anne

"Neil and I were both politically active and worked together in study groups, as well as the Vietnam and student movements, and one of the main characteristics of the relationship was his political education of me. A twist to this though was that I found it impossible to work politically on my own, and that the political and emotional relations were so much part of each other that all sorts of problems emerged. My lack of political independence was one aspect of this. I experienced working politically where I was teaching as an attack on him, and in conflict with our relationship. But he didn't experience it in the same way if he or I were working independently. It seems as though I had acquired my political identity with the emotional relationship, and that the two went together so that to change one involved challenging the other; and that the two didn't go together in the same way for him as for me. I had acquired my political views from him, going to meetings was part of the relationship, as was making derisory comments about political groups we disagreed with. I always referred to him for affirmation when I'd extrapolated from his views to a new area, and often didn't know whether I held the views because I believed in them or because he did. I used to forget what 'we' thought was wrong with IS, and where surplus-value came from.

I don't think that over that period I thought separately from Neil at all. So as soon as I did, and began to act independently, I felt it was an attack on him — which it was objectively for me, as it challenged the way my political identity was tied up with him. Then I started establishing personal relationships with the people I was working politically with, so that they became an alternative network of people, in conflict with our common friends. This independence made me feel that I didn't need him any more. within the kind of wanting versus not wanting a relationship dilemma I was in at that time. By 'independence' I don't mean to suggest that we should have ceased to work with each other, but that through being involved with others, there was the possibility of developing political ideas not exclusively within the relationship.

A second area of problems was the conflict that arises directly out of not separating out or being able to identify as specific, the political and emotional parts of the relationship. For example, there were occasions when I became neurotic when he went out to meetings late in the evening, or stayed out duplicating after I had gone to bed. I used to get very screwed up if he didn't come back before I went to bed, and started behaving in a very wifely way, ringing him up every few minutes. I just used to get annoyed, not really knowing why. I would never deliberately or consciously have said that I didn't want him to go out on his own, although on reflection, this is what my annoyance indicated. This lack of differentiation between emotional and political had bad effects for both. As personal and political commitment seemed to go together for me, they were either both with him, or both without him, so that political independence entailed a real emotional withdrawal."

You can see from these personal accounts that there are different strands for each of us in the relation between politics and sexuality, and that it is different for the man than for the women. To some extent, for all of us the contradiction involved the relation between intellectuality and sexuality. This was because our politics was too much contained within intellectual activity, particularly in our early involvement in the student movement. And because as people who had been highly educated for years and years, ideas had played a real and deeply felt part in our formation and identities. In this respect, the politics had similar dissociated relations to the family as does the politics of the left groups, in two related ways: insofar as it was a politics external to personal things, and insofar as theory was something done by individuals. This was more true of the man; the women were struggling with some ideas about the politics of the personal. But for us all, the context of the individual production of theory made it contradictory to put any such ideas into practice in our actual personal relationships.

The way the left groups make politics sometimes external to personal relationships of their activists isn't quite the same dissociation as between parliamentary politics and the family, because left groups contain ideas that are potentially more antagonistic to the personal relationship: the ideas at least assume the collective development of relations and theory, even if the group's practice does not.

Changing the basis of our relationships

Turning now to the practice 'on ourselves', we shall give some examples of how, within the particular sexual relationships we are involved in, we have tried to change the interconnection between sexual, political and domestic relations.

What each of us is doing overall differs between individuals, as does the way the relationships fit into our lives. Our overall situation is not the same in that we work separately as well as together, we have our own friends, and we have different living situations. We shall concentrate on the sexual and political aspects of the relationships themselves, however, as the linkage between these two aspects has been most contradictory in this context in the past.

We are not trying to write as one person, although the experience is a collective one, nor to give a total account. The purpose of writing about what we have done is to show how we have challenged, to a limited extent, the way different types of relations tend to get interfused in the family and in the couple, and to show how our theory has come out of our practice.

The context. There are three of us: two women, and a man. The women both have a sexual relationship with the man, but these started at different times and on different bases. We did not decide on principle that there should be three of us, nor to be heterosexual. This particular combination of relationships is the only one we can write about at present.

At the beginning the situation was very different from now. One of us was also involved with somebody else, and hoped to be able to work things out with him. The women did not know each other at all and thought that having a relationship with the same man was in itself not a very good reason for getting to know each other. Also at the beginning the two relationships were quite separate: we met mainly in the two's, and each 'couple' was a separate focus of political discussion and emotional relating. We were not all working together politically, but it was largely because there were two separate political agreements as to the possibilities of working out a sexual politics within each relationship that it was subsequently made possible to develop a more collective politics. But to begin with that was something to be proved.

We all wanted to get out of the couple situation, and to avoid the emotional aspect of the relationships becoming the base of all our activities. But the relationship between politics and sex was very different in the two relationships: Anne and Pete had had a relationship for about eighteen months, but had stopped sleeping together. Mary and Pete had been friends for some time but only recently started having a sexual relationship.

Political and sexual relations

The problem in each of the two's was to articulate the different aspects of the relationship with each other, notably politics and sex. And overall, between the three of us, we had to decide how the two sexual relationships would relate to each other, and what sort of relationship we wanted there to be between the three of us, between the two women, and in the two's, politically, sexually, and domestically. The politics here is of two sorts: sexual politics within the relationships, and our other political work. So in talking of political relations between us, we mean how we've been trying to work out political struggles in jobs, education, and women's groups.

As there was a large measure of political agreement between us anyway, we decided early on to try to work collectively and politically both in the group and between the three of us, and over time the couple has lost its salience as a focus of politics. This is why in explaining how we changed the relationship between politics and sex in the two's, we are writing about how we have constructed the relationship between the three of us, as that was the context and the unit in which we were able to act on the way the different relations interacted. The couples ceased to be the basic unit of all activity as we came to work together more collectively. In the couple, the sexual relationship had been the framework within which everything else had basically taken place. Now, the three is more like the framework, the overall structure, within which the sexual relations between the two's had a specific place, worked out collectively. Because of this we have been able to reflect on how the different relations, political and sexual, are 'normally' related to each other in the family or couple.

This doesn't mean that we don't work or do politics in the two's. We do. Nor does it mean that the three of us are a political unit. It is rather that our political work (in the women's liberation movement, at work, in education, etc.) articulates with sex and emotions in a very different way from before. There aren't separate bonds with a separate existence, but we are able to identify the different aspects that go to make up a relationship, and this questions what it is to have 'a relationship'.

At the beginning there were two separate 'relationships', and this could in itself have led to conflict: it put the relationship between the women on an entirely different basis from the two sexual relationships, and gave prominence to the heterosexuality of the situation, and to the man. Also, because of the way the political relations were still tied up with the sexual ones, the sexual-personal basis of each relationship was somehow more salient that the political one. We knew it would be disastrous if we ended up with two separate and parallel couples each relating emotionally and politically, or if the only contact between them was through the man who could thereby become the pivotal figure, and in a position to dominate.

So we had to construct the relationship between the three of us (which was then between the two two's) in just as deliberate and conscious way as in the two's, and with just as much discussion about what we wanted to achieve and why and how. We did not know in advance how not to be couples, and we went very slowly and carefully, getting to know each other better, working together in the group, developing some trust in each other through out commitment to sexual politics and to not wanting a couple situation. We paid a lot of attention to arrangements, which we decided collectively, to deciding who should see who when, and what priority should be given to meeting in the three or in the two.

There are two main ways we have tried to change the original two's. Firstly, the women have worked out a relationship with each other, and now work and act together and independently from Pete (see on). Secondly, there has been a major shift in which the three has become perhaps the more central unit for each of us rather than the two two's.

The decisions and discussions about how to construct the relations, about 'arrangements', are only superficially about actual arrangements. They are really attempts to work out what we were trying to do in being together and in breaking out of the couple, and how to do it, rather than pragmatic arrangements to avoid conflict.

For example, we decided that Mary and Pete would not sleep together at all for the first few months, at least six, for reasons to do with the overall situation as well as the relationship between themselves. This was because Anne and Pete had to work out a sexual relationship that had become difficult in the year previously, and Mary and the man she was then living with needed the space to try to sort out the problems between them. There would have been little chance of the different sexual relations working out unless there was this space. Another thing was that there was a danger at the beginning that the way the relationship between Mary and Pete had started — as a sexual relationship without much worked out practically about how they could work together politically — would make it difficult for them to avoid the old patterns of feeling being set up. This was done to make it more possible for them to be more conscious of what was happening, and not to let the sexual relationships become the main basis for wanting to work together politically, and among the three of us.

Another area of collective decision was how often to see each other in the two's, how often in the three, and what were the priorities. We didn't want a situation where we felt that we were only 'really' seeing each other when we were in the two's, or being in the three to feel like a substraction from the 'real' relationships. The more we had real reasons for being together as a three, like working or writing, the more this has ceased to be a problem. Usually we see each other in the two's twice a week, but if there are lots of meetings, or things that we need to discuss between the three urgently, we reduce this. We found that sticking rigidly to a twice-a-week routine doesn't make sense if there are things to be sorted out that we are all involved in; the two's feel peculiar being together at those times anyway. As we don't live together, we have to decide in advance when we are going to see each other, so it's not like being together all the time except when we are doing something else, as in a couple living together. The sexual relations do not operate as a home background for us in the same way that they had before.

Another thing we have had to sort out is how we relate to each other as a three. When we are together as a three we don't express ourselves sexually as when we are alone in the two's. For example, we decided that we would not sleep together in couples when we were all together in the same place over night, after a meeting, when we have been working or on holiday together. To revert to the sexual relationship would have been like saying that the sexual basis was the most salient, and it was not something any of us would have felt at ease doing. So when we are together, we try to relate as a three rather than as two sexual sub-units.

Another area we have had to work out is how to operate when

there are disagreements or conflicts between two or three of us, or when there are emotional crises. We've tried to discuss the disagreements for what they are, and decide what it would mean for us to go on sleeping together in the two's before it has been fully sorted out. If the conflict is between the two women, or between one of the women and Pete, then sleeping with Pete could become a competitive or antagonistic act between the women, or a way of solidarising with Pete against the other woman, or for the other woman to suspect this even if it wasn't the case; or finally, a way of using the emotional relationship to gloss over political conflict. We couldn't expect never to have political disagreements, but the problems of how they get intermingled with the emotional relations became obvious as there were three of us. In the couple, as we suggested earlier, either the two relations, political and sexual, are so dissociated that political disagreement doesn't affect sex, or they are so integrated that any political difference constitutes an enormous challenge to the relationship, or sex becomes a way of cooling out the conflict. We have tried to struggle against all of these possibilities, and also against the possibility of one sexual relationship working against the other through this dynamic.

These decisions, arrangements and routines are difficult to describe. They are not rules, or repressive measures that we have invented to control ourselves or have erected against our feelings. On the contrary, we have treated our anxieties and fears about the situation as real worries to be confronted, rather than repressed, as we hope also to show in the section on sexuality. These arrangements were more ways of working out how to construct the relationship between the two two's that retained the closeness of the two's and the solidarity of the three, but where the sexual relationship wouldn't be the pivot of everything. They changed the basis of our feelings for each other as the two's ceased to be in any sort of conflict with the three. As there was no set way of behaving or conducting relationships for us all to fall into, we had to work out everything and construct the principles, and this meant working out what we wanted to do in being together, rather than just establishing a modus vivendi.

So, we've tried to construct consciously an overall structure of the way we relate to each other, in which the sexual relations have a specific link with what we are doing politically. Because political decisions about how we should relate are taken as a three, this has shifted the centre of the political relations from the two's and focused it more in the three and in the group. This in turn has meant a displacement of the whole centrality of emotions and sex within the personal relations, partly because sexuality is one of the main areas we have been engaged on a common political project over. The sexual-emotional relations are much more just one aspect of the way we relate to each other overall, rather than being the pivotal basis of all other relations. The practical decisions are about the specific political problems of the place of sexual relations in the overall structure of our relations.

These changes have not been brought about easily, and in turn they raise further problems and worries. For example, when we have been a lot together in the three, the only reason for being in the two's sometimes seems to be to have sex, making sex into something dissociated, but in a different way, from political relations. This has been particularly the case when we've been working together all day, say in a rush to get a pamphlet done. It really feels odd to be left together in a two then. But it's not really as if there were a political relationship between some people, and completely separate sexual relations with other people. We are the same people but in different contexts. Why this seems odd is because in trying to construct the overall structure of political and sexual relations, we have unsettled the 'relationship'. We have thought about what relations go into making a relationship between two people, and replaced the idea of an undifferentiated unity with that of different and specific relations that articulate with each other in any one 'relationship'. From this point of view, the main thing seems to be the different relations, and the relationship becomes an empirical conglomerate of the different relations.

We have found thinking about it quite anxiety-provoking and insecure-making. In the course of changing things, we run the risk of not knowing what to put in their place, for example, not knowing what sex is about or for, and being disoriented about it. In emphasising the specificity of the relations we haven't really found a way of describing the synthesis, the articulation and how the relations are felt to integrate. So also the understanding of it theorises something which we may have already partly worked out in practice, but not given a name to, and somehow realising this provokes insecurities even when what we are doing in practice does not.

Relations between women

Anne and Mary

"Here we are going to talk about the political relationship between women, 'sisterhood'. What we'll be talking about is how to work out political relations between women if their main sexual commitment is to men. Having a sexual relation with the same man brought up for us the general problems of political and emotional relations between women who are heterosexual in a particularly acute way. It's just that when women relate to the same man it brings out into the open a lot of the underlying relations between women which you don't see when each woman has a separate man.

Women in general are divided and separated from each other in society because each woman is basically identified with her own man, or would like to be. This isn't just a question of the psychology of women, and inner hostilities to each other; it's a social structure where sexuality is based on the couple and the family.

When heterosexual women meet in the women's movement, say in consciousness-raising groups, we aren't with our individual men. It is possible for sisterly solidarity to develop among women on their own, which can carry on because it isn't threatened by the dependence on men, competition for men, and idealisation of men, which can all happen outside. Some consciousness-raising groups have a kind of female solidarity based almost entirely on sympathy and understanding for each other's difficulties as women in relationships to men, without actually being able to challenge the basic situation. Sometimes the fact that everyone in the room is deeply committed to a particular man or men, is hardly mentioned. It all goes on in parallel.

So in a way, the political relation between women is ambiguous when there is this split between the movement and our individual private lives. Men are in the background of the movement, but in the foreground of the lives of many of us. This provides an underlying structure to the relationships between women, which isn't immediately obvious when we are together as women. This concealment means that we can have a kind of abstract emotional feeling for each other at meetings and conferences, that feels quite strong and warm, but which can easily evaporate or turn into hostility if the special relationship with the man is really threatened. One effect of this is that emotional relationships, feelings between women, such as liking, have sexual overtones to do with women's relationships with men. The relationships with men are hidden when women are alone together, and so the origin of some of those feelings can be avoided. We, in our relationships to Pete, couldn't so easily avoid it — it was very obvious that our feelings towards each other came partly from the way we were each involved with a man, and not only from our relationship to each other.

Both of us had a general political and personal commitment to working out this sexual situation because of our past experience of being in couples and seeing that as connected with the oppression of women. But although there was this political commitment to each other, we didn't want to get emotionally close just by laying down that we should be or to make the sexual set-up work. We didn't think that would be feasible anyway, because of all sorts of insecurity and jealousy we were feeling to start with. To begin with, we didn't really know what to do. We didn't know each other at all. We both felt quite wary, even resentful, of the idea that we should get to know each other because of him. We couldn't start by taking for granted any easy mutual liking, like a usual friendship, because there were too many mixed and uncomfortable feelings coming from our separate involvements with him. It was easy to pick on some

82

difference or disagreement between the two of us as a reason for feeling that we couldn't possibly get on together; little things over which we jarred, which with anyone else would pass by as some small irritant, would make us feel disproportionately angry or afraid or suspicious.

It wasn't just disagreements, but ways of acting, feeling, and expressing ourselves that we became watchful for. There were big differences of temperament and in the directness with which we revealed our emotions, that made us feel that if we had met each other independently, we would have found it hard even to have got close enough to know each other very well. At the beginning, when each of our relationships to the man was pretty opaque to the other, these differences in what we were like were threatening. But at the same time, we were talking and working together, all trying to work out what the basis of a general sexual and feminist politics could be, and how our own personal sexual relations fitted into that. We listened and learned about each other's pasts, each other's ways of reacting in the present, and gradually we saw how we each had become the way we are.

The more we realised these things, the less we felt the differences as personal attacks, or as fixed attributes of each other that we could just react to — she is like this, she is like that. We were trying to change a lot of the ways we feel and do things anyway, and we were able to take a much more comradely approach to what each other was like, and this has made us closer to each other in a different way than liking.

This experience has made us realise how individualistic a basis for a relationship 'liking' can be. It often rests on similarities of emotional styles and reinforces the self-image or identity of each person. It can also be brutal and divisive: liking can be like judging and assessing — you respond to people whose qualities you 'like', in the same way as you respond to people sexually who you deem are 'attractive'. Our own feelings of being threatened by the differences between us, made us think how much women's constructed images of themselves, including clothes, really are a threat to relations between them, even when women are alone together; for, the look of approval from men is still there even when men in body aren't. The orientation to men is the source of the images, ideals and standards that affect how women feel about each other.

But the main thing we realised from our experience as a thing to be changed, was the split between our sexual commitment to men, and political commitment as women. As long as each woman was working out her sexual and emotional relationship with the man separately and privately, then this would be the hidden source of whatever the feelings were between the two women.

One of the main things we thought right at the beginning was that the two women and one man situation could be the most sexist of all arrangements, and just make even more extreme the problems we'd felt in a private love relationship before. This would happen if the two sexual relationships were kept apart, and there were no shared knowledge and criteria for what everyone was doing. If the two sexual relationships were kept basically private from each other, each with their own validity over which the other had no claims, each with a special exclusive 'magic', then we would have to act individually, and this would give control to the man, or to whichever of the women had the advantage, usually the latest to arrive. If the two sexual relationships aren't worked out in common, each individual has to manipulate and scheme, and either calculates to his or her advantage, or to adapt to the others. So right from the start, we saw personal and political reasons why the two sexual relationships should be brought into a conscious and worked out relation to each other.

This particular experience of ours makes us want to make the general point that mistrust and lack of longterm commitment between women comes from the private and world-of-their-own character of sexual love relationships, which prevents women making political relations with each other and prevents heterosexual women from developing emotional relationships that really do arise from what we are doing politically together as women.

As long as there is no collective working out of our sexual relationships with men, by the women in the movement, we remain with our political and sexual commitments split and set against each other. We're not sure what this means in practice for the movement, whether it means mixed groups like the one we've been in as well as women's groups, or what. It is a problem we need to discuss more in the women's movement."

Sexual and domestic relations

So far we have explained the relation between sex and politics for us. Turning now to the other relation that we examined in the capitalist family, sex and economics, the three of us do not live together, are financially independent and do not constitute a domestic economy. There are several things we mean by domestic economy.

Firstly living together. We think that living with the people you are sexually involved with carries the danger that the sexual relationship can become the pivot of all other activities, and the base from which all other relations automatically follow: political, economic and domestic. In turn sharing a domestic economy has a determining effect on how sexual relationships are worked out; it is very difficult to take an independent stance from the relationship if you are always within it, and there is the pressure to sort out problems and conflicts as quickly as possible to avoid tension in a living situation. One of us had been previously in a semi-commune. There hadn't been any particular reason for a domestic set-up to emerge from the emotional relations in the first place. But more important, as soon as intractable emotional problems arose, one person after another moved out. This meant that a decision to change the basis of emotional relations also implied a complete change in living situation, and showed how unworked out the relation between domestic-economic and sexual relations was.

All our upbringing conditions us to link up emotions and domestic relations in the same locus — the home; and it is really the 'home' as the heart of the family that we have questioned. We didn't think that we would be able to sort out these relations from each other or solve the problem of how to link them up within a communal situation, so we have taken the rather crude step of separating them out, by none of us living together. None of us has a very satisfactory living situation, but we have put the sexual relations in a different relation to meetings, work, and everything else we are doing, and have avoided the personal relationships becoming an emotional retreat from the world via the home.

Secondly, the domestic economy is a unit of consumption based on individual wage labour, and is a unit for the reproduction of labour power, especially the rearing of children. The choices of political action to change the relation between these and sexual relations are necessarily limited by the extent to which the economic relations of capitalism are themselves unchanged. Although we have not set up the same kinds of links between sexual and economic relations as exist in the family, this doesn't change our dependence on wage labour, nor the individualised domestic economy. It only means that these are no longer coterminous with sexual relations. We are each economically independent of each other, and there is no sexual division of labour between us. But while it is important that the women are financially independent of the man, we don't consider the fact that this means we are each individual wage labourers now very progressive. Communes can change the relations of the domestic economy from within to some extent if economies of scale mean that not everyone needs to work; so can squats where the absence of rent also diminishes the dependence on a wage. But to change the economic relations to which our personal relations articulate, requires a revolution in consumption and in the mode of reproduction of labour power overall.

None of us has children, and if we had, our living situation and economic relations would have been much more problematic. Clearly the domestic economy won't be changed until there is a social alternative to the nuclear family as the place for bringing up children, and until children are no longer the sole responsibility of their parents, and particularly their mothers.

The fact that we haven't written much about children doesn't mean that we don't think that a political relation to children isn't crucial. Personally we don't have experience of how having children changes domestic, political and emotional relations, and hope that those who have will write about it. But it does seem that any political and revolutionary group — including ours if we had people with children — would have to work out a sexual politics which included decisions as to how, and within what kinds of domestic set-up, to relate to children. Otherwise there would be no possibility of a generalised political struggle against the existing capitalist family.

SEX AND SEXUALITY

So far we have talked about the way sexuality fits with other social relations. In this section we are going to talk more specifically about how this makes us look at sex and sexuality. By 'sex' we mean the social forms of physical interaction; and by 'sexuality' we mean the whole complex of sexual love relationships that were the subject of the first pamphlet (the givenness, individualism, abstractness of feelings, and so on); so what we say here should be seen in the context of what we said there — we don't think it possible to change the emotional basis of the couple without changing the kind of sex that goes with those emotions. We have talked about putting political relations into a new relation with sexual relations; making sex a specific relation; constructing the sexual relation. Now we ask the question, which is a practical-political as well as a theoretical problem, What is the sexual relation? What is sex?

Sex is, and always has been, a form of social relation for human beings. In the past, it has usually taken place in the context of reproduction. As sex has become detached from reproduction with the use of contraceptives, this is no longer the major social determining context of sex. This means that there is now a historical question as to what sex is, not just a theoretical question or a question of definition. In a way, it is because the old social relation doesn't hold that we are faced with the confusion about what sex is, which is really a question of what sex could be, what social relation we wish to make out of sex. We ourselves feel this now as an experience of strangeness and uncertainty in making love, the more we have disturbed our own habitual contexts and emotional habits.

Sex is one of the ways we relate to others with our bodies. It is only part of our physical relation with the world, both how we relate to our own bodies, and other people's. There are social forms within which any physical relation or activity takes place, whether it be eating, exercising, dancing, dressing or sex. Different societies have different social forms within which physical relations occur. Libertarian sexual ideologies often include abstract injunctions to touch each other more, to be 'natural' or 'spontaneous', as well as to have more sex as such. This over-rides the problems about the social forms of physicality: people's social relation to their own bodies is already very complicated and cannot be changed by simple wish, prescription, or invocation to nature. In our society, the work ethic and the daily organisation of work deeply affect people's physicality, limiting the physical relations to very small times and places, sometimes limiting the physical interaction of people, and sex, to just fantasy, so that some people can only dream and imagine touching each other. Indeed, not just some people: there is big business based on the containment of sex to fantasy.

The introduction of widespread contraception and the possibility of freeing sex from reproduction actually leaves sex within other complex social forms; it is only made to appear to shed its social forms and to be now a purely physical function, a physical interaction. This is perhaps because contraception is a physical measure, and so conceals the social relations it creates. So the ideal of physical interaction in sex, an ideal which characterises both permissive bourgeois culture and libertarian sexual politics, is an idea separated from any idea of the general social development of the context of physical activity and interaction. If the social forms are left unchanged, physical contact takes on existing social forms: so, for example, 'touching' other people more can be a power relation.

The point is, the physical isn't just physical, but is always social-physical. The way that we, in this and the previous pamphlet, have analysed the entanglement of sex with the given feelings of the family can perhaps lead to a kind of misunderstanding about sex as purely physical. Disentangling sex from this kind of emotionality can seem to leave it as 'just' physical interaction. And yet we know for ourselves that we are not having sex as just a kind of body contact, a simple sensationism, but a complex emotional social and physical activity together. Feelings of physical sexual pleasure are not given tactile sensations always and every-where the same: touching has different significances, feels different, in different contexts of relations. So 'good sex' isn't a question of physical techniques, but of the whole social form in which people make love. A politics of sex, as only one part of a politics of sexual relationships as a whole, would have to consider what kinds of social relations touching and other body activities can be.

Reich and Freud have a biologism about sex that we reject. It is obviously true that human beings are biological organisms. Being a biological organism means having physical activities and relations in the world, including eating and sex. This is true of all biological organisms. On it, Freud and Reich base their ideas that sexual activity is an instinct. But the facts of eating and sex are not instincts in human beings, even if they are attributes of the biological organism.

An instinctual action is one that is entirely under biological, physical, control. So the way an animal's eating behaviour is governed is largely instinctual. Similarly with sex in animals. But in human beings, although biological, neither eating nor sex are under biological control, but are social and therefore historical relations. That a person eats is a fact of being a biological organism which needs to eat. But how — and for many people, whether — they eat, is not at all under biological control. There is no instinctual given for how people survive physically in the world (both diet and cooking being social), nor how they relate physically to each other. And just being physically existent is a tautological biological fact, not an instinctual one.

Therefore, how we are physically sexual is socially formed; and if we are to look at the ways we are going to change being sexual, it is in ways which have implications for the general social forms of being sexual. There is no natural instinctual given to fall back on, or to emerge from some animal place 'beneath' social conditioning. Sexuality isn't to be thought of as socially 'conditioned' in the sense that individuals learn behaviour that overlays and suppresses their natural sexuality. Rather a person's own individual sexuality is formed as one instance of the general structural character of social sexual relations. These social relations must be struggled with, and new ones formed, to form new modes of being sexual. We can't just individually break out of old patterns. Libertarian ideologies of releasing natural sexual energy make the profoundly anti-political assumption that the individual, with his or her inner instincts, inner nature, could be the source of a new mode of sexuality, a purely individual liberation from the repressive relations of the present society.

This is the background to our conception of constructing sex and sexuality, rather than expressing sex. Constructing sex does not mean as between us as individuals. The political problem is to construct the general social forms of physical sexual interaction. Our practice on ourselves is only a very limited and partial way of working out what that politics and theory could be.

These general thoughts about sex came up as we reflected on what we were doing about sex within each of the two relationships. What now follows is a mix of theory with accounts of the experiences written by different people.

Constructing sex

Anne

"Our relationship had become unstuck by one aspect being screwy, that is, sex. At the time, it seemed peculiar that we could be very close politically, find it easy to talk to each other, be each other's closest friend for a long time, at the same time as becoming increasingly sexually estranged. We didn't want to stop being close friends and comrades just because of problems of sex.

We tried to analyse how we had come to be so physically 'incompatible', which is what it seemed like — having different ways of touching and expressing affection, or different ways of physically relating. We worked out what kind of differences the differences were, what aspects of the other's behaviour we couldn't relate to, and then tried to understand how each of us had come to have that way of relating. We saw a lot of it as due to our family pasts in that our patterns of expression were ones which had been formed in the family, and then, that when these differences were put into relation to each other, they exacerbated the original differences.

He had been within a framework of taking feelings and sexual attraction as given, and in his marriage had tried to create a totally self-sufficient loving couple, as atmospheric as his family had been, with sex as a striving for unconscious unity and as symbolic of the strength of feelings. This made him worry that he didn't have 'enough' feelings for me, and together with feeling sexually inadequate, this made him very unsure about why we were sleeping together and what sex was, making him timid, apparently 'repressed', yet unable to say what the problem was as he feared this would be an emotional attack on me. At the same time, I behaved physically in a rather defensive way, affectionately rather than sexually, unable to express what I really felt. I thought that if I did expose my feelings I would make myself vulnerable to attack. It wasn't that I didn't want to be close, but I didn't know how to be.

Over time, my relationships had led to a split between the way I expressed myself emotionally and sexually. My overt expression of emotion was through a cuddly kind of affection, whereas I treated sex as a purely physical thing, to experience physical pleasure, the main aim being to get as excited as possible and have as many orgasms as possible. In these terms, sex with Pete was alright at first, but quite soon, my and his differences interacted with each other so that the whole thing became quite grotesque with me wanting to all the time and him being paranoid about me.

The way we came to understand the differences highlighted the way we had reproduced the relationships in our childhood families in our adult sexual relationships. My emotional needs, the way I wanted to be cuddled, my shame at my body, came straight out of my relationship with my parents. The way I felt insecure if a particular form of affection wasn't shown must have something to do with the notable absence of overt sex in the family, and with the highly sub-sexual way my father related to me. To become sexual would involve a break with my family, and specifically with my father, and this was not a step I had made in a physical sense even if for years I had virtually nothing to do with my parents. It's not that I hadn't broken with them, but that I still carried within me ways of acting that I had had with them but wasn't aware of.

We have theorised the couple largely as reproducing emotional needs and modes of gratification formed in the family. So breaking out of the couple also implies creating an alternative to the family. No doubt, most people avoid the impasse I was in by recreating the family in their couple, becoming sexual with someone who acts for their parents. For me, the contradiction between being affectionate and sexual, was never overcome by integrating these in a couple. So in constructing the relationship with Pete, I seem to have passed straight from the type of emotional relation with parents to a more consciously worked out relation between sex and emotions, without passing through the stage of a fantasy relation of the loving couple.

But that this still involved breaking with the family was indicated a few months later when Pete and Mary started sleeping together, which I experienced as them being the adults and me as the child. I had constant dreams in which they were the parents, or were in various kinds of blood relation to me which precluded a sexual relationship between me and Pete, but not between them. Obviously the situation was not like that, but I often dream things in their most extreme just when I am getting out of them, and this seemed to indicate a final break with my family.

In talking about these differences, we were able to change the way we acted. The aim was not to obliterate differences and arrive at some common denominator way of acting which we could both tolerate. It was more questioning why we should just behave on the basis of unconsciously formed ways of physically relating. This was quite difficult and painful, given the ingrainedness of our socially formed ways of physically relating connected with familial type emotions, requiring a strongly felt common commitment to change things and work them out, rather than from any direct expression of sexual feelings — which would have been impossible. On the other hand, this also meant that it was impossible for sex to be used symbolically for other things if it was going badly. This was because of the context of constructing the relation between relations, sorting out what was specifically sexual, political, emotional, etc.

At the time, we didn't know whether we would be able to work anything out sexually, only that it would be very distressing for some time delving into the past, analysing our physical moves, and saying what actions on the part of the other person made us anxious. I got out of the physical sensation syndrome. Sex became much more an explicitly social physical relation, responding to, and changing, how the other person had been socially formed to relate physically, rather than trying to achieve the, in fact, equally social, aims of individual/mutual 'purely physical', ecstasy; e.g. 'genital satisfaction'.

I'm sure that Pete and I were able to construct a sexual relationship like this only because we had made a commitment not based on given sexual feelings, questioning our socially given ways of behaving, and re-thought how sex had functioned in relation to emotions as symbolic of them. If the relationship is seen as a complex of different relations, the relation between which is to be constructed, and not around sexual attraction as a symbol of emotions, then it needn't stand or fall with sex, and that makes it more possible to act constructively towards sex."

Changing the place of sex

Mary

"This is about how I tried to change the way in which I had always used sex as a special close relationship, where my identity would depend on his feelings for me.

The six months or so that Pete and I weren't sleeping together meant that I had to find other solutions to emotional problems than dissolving them in the closeness of sex. We really had to confront differences between us, and areas of unknowns, and we had to work out our political and other social relations at their own level, not just making them aspects of the sexual and emotional closeness. The deliberate distance we set did have its problems too. It itself became the cause of some old feelings I had been prone to with men: the decision not to make love would start to seem like some externally imposed taboo, sometimes, imposed by him on me. I would then worry that he didn't like me enough. I needed proof of his feelings for me in a more direct emotional way than the commitment I knew he had to what we were doing overall. I wasn't used to not getting a very direct intuitive emotional response, nor had I ever had to consider before whether to act on my own immediate feelings. It all made me very anxious and insecure. I realised how much I depended on the constant reassurance that I was loved and liked for myself, and that this was to be expressed in sexual attraction to me.

The fact that we were so committed to each other politically, trusted each other, wasn't to the point of these feelings. I still had a tendency to need the 'magic spell' of love to feel secure, whatever else was also being securely worked out. I discovered that I didn't completely understand or trust a relationship where I didn't feel there was an over-riding attraction for what I was like as its basis. I was not directly very jealous, but the quality of emotional dialogue that I needed was something that can only be between two people who are special for each other. This implies that there should not be another sexual relationship of equal stature, even though that didn't figure in the way I actually felt about it.

This has changed, partly as I've come to understand from my past why I take this form of relationship so much for granted; and also because as I've come to understand the other side to it, the blocks on other activities, acting and thinking about other things, because my attention is so much in a dialogue with the person I'm sexually involved with. Seeing the processes of thought and feeling that underlie these problems has made it progressively easier not to live the entanglements so unconsciously, and easier not to repeat it again and again.

The changes did not occur by just talking, and understanding the basis of the problems did not happen just by talking either. Both occurred because of the actual political contexts and arrangements we created for the sexual relations."

About having two sexual relationships

Pete

"Although I have tried to work out problems about sex in two sexual relations, I do not think that the political problems are peculiar to this situation, and I shall first look at the problems, and then go on to look at the way they affected the relation between the two sexual relations.

I think it would be a form of individualism if I had just taken sexual feelings and modes of expression as a given thing going on between me and another person. There would be bound to be differences between the two sexual relationships, and these differences if taken as given, would have been a basis, I think, for real and genuine antagonisms. But the basic problem is not that given differences would become a basis for antagonisms, but that within each relationship nothing could have been worked out about what sex was about, or what relation sex had to other aspects of the relationships, if sexual feelings had been taken as just given, part of a personality.

Now, the reason why I could begin to work out some of these problems was not so much that I had sexual feelings, started a sexual relationship, and then worked out sex. The reason for starting a sexual relationship was much more feeling there was a mutual interest in working out problems of sex that had beset us in the past, i.e., being engaged in some kind of sexual struggle from the beginning.

This is particularly true granted the state I had been in. I had been in a relationship with Anne that had ceased to be sexual during which I had become physically paranoid. For a year I had been incapable of anything but a kind of fear of sex and pretty well all physical contact. I had experienced this as some kind of psychological hang-up, as being repressed, and as being incapable of having any feelings — very much within the bourgeois ideology of 'having feelings', and of 'personality characteristics'.

This changed through being able to see that sexual relationships need not be based on 'having' or 'not having' sexual feelings of attraction, in the sense of being turned on by someone and going to bed. Instead it was possible to see how a sexual relationship could be consciously constructed with an idea about what we wanted to make sex be about — not to rely on natural spontaneity which had been so unhelpful an ally in the past. To begin with, I had been able to think this on starting a new sexual relationship with Mary. But looking at it like this, it was important that I could envisage the possibility of overcoming sexual paranoia in my relationship with Anne — solving sexual problems politically in a general way wasn't to be a question of changing particular sexual partners. For, it would have been very much taking sexual feelings as given if I had simply, as I had up to that point, acted on given feelings of paranoia.

So in talking about what we were trying to achieve in sex, what kind of relation, and what its relation was to other relations, and seeing how it was that the actual ways we had of acting sexually had generated a sexual problem, the paranoia was gradually overcome. By sexual ways of acting, I don't of course mean techniques. I mean such things as ways of expressing affection which have been formed in the family, as well as certain cultural images of sexual ecstasy one might be trying to imitate or feel judged by. Some of these ways of acting physically (hugging, kissing) are loaded with emotional meanings they had from the ways that mothers and fathers had of acting physically towards us as children. These were profoundly ambivalent, since they contain in their origin a taboo against direct sexual expression: I have felt that some of these experiences of affection are, coming from me, more defences against sexuality, or at least have an uncertain relation to it. They are connected with all kinds of other things that might be being aimed at in the relationship, special kinds of closeness.

As for some of the cultural images, I mean such things as striving for total unity in mutual ecstasy (which had been important in my head) — which I now think is just a way for men having the illusion that ecstasy is mutual. What I mean by this is that physiological differences in the way men have orgasms, erections, and penetration, does make it easier for men to have the illusion that mutual ecstasy is coterminous with their physiological excitement. Such images have obscured for me the whole fact that the sensual feelings of men and women are different, owing to biological differences, and cannot be experienced directly at all, let alone be mutual. Although heterosexual, I now wonder more what heterosexuality is when for a long time I don't think I recognised the radical physical dissimilarity between the sexes in my striving for total unification in sex.

Cultural images, such as striving for unity, of being one with another, are cultural and ideological things. But they also relate to the ways of physically expressing affection that come from relations to parents: here the actual differences between the sexes in the physical expressions of affection, son-mother, father-daughter, are normally underplayed through the absence of any explicitly heterosexual interaction. This is only questioning the relation between physical expression and sexuality within heterosexuality. It's not intended to give a privileged position to that.

A further cultural image is a kind of orgasm fetishism, in which the aim of sexual interaction is to have an orgasm; as if the aim was not inter-action, but for a person to 'have an orgasm', or to achieve some kind of physical state. This makes it very difficult to see sex as a social relation at all. As an image I had been trying to live up to, it contributed to not being able to think about sex except as something both private and individual in essence, completely dissociated from everything that went on out of bed. Through this kind of image, sex could and did acquire a privilege over all other aspects of relationships as the specially close form of personal contact. As such it would be impossible to put into a political relation with other relations, or indeed to have a politics of sexuality at all.

What we have tried to do instead is to try to work out some kind of common principles about what sex was about, so that having sex was more a kind of sexual agreement than a relation based on given sexual feelings of arousal. The physical relations had a place within the overall structure of what we each were trying to do. As such it could not have been done without political agreement on things other than sex. Of course, this means that we are very unsure about what place sex has and also what sex is about, as a social relation. But this is impossible to think about properly at the individual level, between particular people, and would only become clearer in the context of some general struggle to construct different social-physical relations.

Turning now to how this has affected the problems I have had in having two sexual relations, I shall try to say something about what could be called the obverse of jealousy — not that I am claiming that it is any-thing like as hard to bear. But it seems to me in part that jealousy is in part related to a structure of sexual relationships in which each relationship is kept separate, without any common principles about acting on the differences between the sexual relationships. For me, it has always been highly disturbing in my position, when I have gone through periods of not understanding the reasons for the differences in the two relationships, expressed say, in how I have erections or not, whether they occur apparently without much interaction and seem simply to be in a state of arousal or not. I think it is in these periods when the differences have been vaguely understood and are difficult to act on and change, that sex seems to have been most given. It made me feel sexually schizoid, not knowing what was going on in sex in either relationship.

At these times, I have felt illegitimate both in having any sexual relationship at all, and granted the actual or potential threat of differences between two sexual relationships, particularly illegitimate in having two, since at least some of the anxieties came from having two and the interaction between what was going on in each of them. It has been through trying to understand these kinds of things, and then acting on them so as to make the physical interaction work on the same principles in the two relationships, that some of these things have been changed. This does not mean I was trying to make it the identical physical experience, because each person has had very different sexual formations; so the actual problems were different even if we were trying to develop common theory and method.

Of course, the problem of whether having two sexual relationships is open to becoming sexually schizoid, depends on whether there is a common attempt to work things out, and to discuss what each person is trying to achieve, having a common theory about what sex is about. This is quite different from emotional-sexual individualism, where having more than one relationship could be just having a number of more or less parallel relationships, each independent of, and hidden from, the other. Here differences can be simply compartmentalised, shut off from one another. These are situations like traditional affairs, or purely casual sexual relations, where each sexual relationship can be actively kept separate. Differences have for me become disturbing only by acting on them and confronting them, thinking of them as open to change. This implies that having a politics of sexuality and of sex does mean challenging the ways we have been socially formed to be physical, since the way it is 'naturally' is that sex is made to appear as a physical fact of nature, inherent in each individual biological organism and its physiology. For me, the root of this was that, even in physical interaction and affection in the family past, physical interaction was cut off from sex, and sex had no social presence."

Jealousy and monogamy

The family creates emotional needs for a kind of sexual love relationship that secures the identity; sex takes place in a structure of relationships in which the relationship between the couple is sharply differentiated from other personal relations, as the inside to the outside. This monogamous structure, and the abstract and individualist feelings on which sexual love is founded, go together (see Pamphlet One). Each person in a couple needs his/her identity affirmed by loving and being loved as he or she was in the family: unconditionally; monogamy allows this need to be fulfilled. Other feelings, the insecurity and aggression of jealousy, are equally the result of needs formed in the family, and are a response to the deviation from monogamy, which prevents their being fulfilled. Jealousy happens because the basis of a person's sexual love relation and identity really is threatened if the other person has a sexual relationship with someone else. As long as sexual relationships are based on the kind of emotional individualism formed in the family, two relationships can only be two competing one-to-one relationships, each with its own inside and outside, each inherently excluding the other, each closed to the other. Or else, the couple is kept central, and the other relationship has the status of an affair, that can perhaps be tolerated provided the person in the secondary relationship accepts that status.

So in setting up a situation as we have, in which there are two women involved with one man, this is itself a structure that creates jealousy, not one which eliminates it. It is just the other side of monogamy. So when we talk about changing the structure of relationships, to change the real basis for jealous feelings, this doesn't mean changing just the formal structure, so that there are three instead of two.

Changing the structure has to involve discovering and changing what there is in the structure which activates the needs which monogamy had hitherto fulfilled. This is something which we couldn't know much about in advance, and we worked things out and altered the way we did things as we went along. One thing that was obvious was that if one relationship was made more central than the other, say by one of the couples living together and the other woman not, that would be a real basis for jealousy in both couples. Another way in which the structure could be characterised is how separate the two sexual relations are kept. The more they are separate, the less they are worked out in common, the more there is real cause for fear and anxiety of being excluded. It would make the women uncertain about their own relationship with the man, and would put the one in the middle in a position of power, whether he wanted it or not.

Here too, making the sexual relationships less separate from each other isn't a formal matter — not just a question of 'reporting' what is 'going on'. Some kinds of sexual relationship which act on the unconsciousness of given feelings, aren't able to be made more open to someone else: it is only possible if within the sexual relationship itself sex is being taken as an area for struggle and change, not just as spontaneous expression of given feelings. Because we tried to understand and work out in practice, in each of the sexual relationships, what the problems were, and ways of being sexual, we gradually found ways of talking about it among the three of us, ways which were aimed at working things out in a common way. This is important because if you just try and report 'facts' which might strain to give an impression as to 'what it's like', this can only feed insecure fantasies, if it is just taken as given facts, not part of a collective working out.

These are examples of what we have tried to do to change the structure of the relationships we are in, and to change the kinds of emotional individualism on which sexual relationships are based. But this isn't all there is to the 'structure'. The structure is a complex interaction of feeling and structure, past and present. The present structure of any specific relationships is actually constituted by the structures of relationships in each of the people's pasts. A family isn't an abstract arrangement of two parents plus one or more children. In different families there are different relationships. The dominant aspect of one child's family may be his or her exclusion from the parents' relationship. This will mean that a present situation of formal exclusion will be felt differently by that person, than by someone whose family was characterised by constant dialogue with the parents. For each of them, a threesome arrangement will be structured differently, will arouse different feelings, will threaten different needs. We have only gradually found out what the structure of our relationship is for each of us, and how the needs of each of us, formed in our different pasts, interact to form what is the specific structure of our three-person situation.

'Jealousy'

Anne

"We think that the ways we've tried to construct the relationships and put them into relation with each other, have laid the structural preconditions for avoiding jealousy. But this doesn't mean that feelings of jealousy just disappear or rather don't appear at all. Sometimes I get very anxious and insecure when I am alone on the nights the other two are sleeping together, either feeling excluded or that secret things are going on that I don't know about. At the beginning, I didn't know how much to think about the other relationship: whether I should always keep in mind that Pete was sexually involved with someone else, or whether I should try to suppress any incipient worries about it and just think about what I was trying to achieve – and I still go through this sometimes. Usually when I'm worrying about something else anyway, or when the three of us have been together a lot and not sleeping with Pete, and then suddenly we (or they) are in the two's again; or when we've had an unsettling discussion about what sex is or something like that. In these circumstances, I tend to lie awake in bed neurotically imagining what is going on, and can't sleep until I'm sure it's all over. This leads quickly to antagonism against Pete on two grounds: that he holds the monopoly of knowledge about the relationships, and however much I am told about what is going on between them, I can't know it directly as he does. This sounds like envy but it's much more an exclusion-and-knowledge thing. And secondly, that it's because of him that I can't sleep and that I'm thinking about him and Mary half the time, instead of the other things I am doing.

We have taken these worries as serious things to be dealt with and

overcome not as anxieties to be repressed. After all, you can only challenge monogamy in practice, and these worries wouldn't have arisen if I'd
been in a monogamous situation. But talking them through has involved
working out ways to talk about sex both in the two's and in the three. If I
just report these worries they become attacks, implying that I don't want
the other two to sleep together. It has taken some time to find a way of
discussing sex and our anxieties about it, and really it is possible only
because of the sort of sex we are trying to construct. If we were each
aiming for magical sex, it would be difficult enough to say anything about
it between sexual partners, even counterproductive, let alone between the
three. If each of us were aiming for the most ecstatic magical sexual
experience, there would have been every reason to be jealous and
threatened, so it is only because of the way we are trying to work out sex
overall that jealousy doesn't just become disruptive or have to be
repressed. In fact, talking through any worries has made me much more
aware of the many-sided nature of their cause, so that while some of the
paradoxes are real ones about being involved with somebody who's
involved with someone else, the way that I experience them has a lot to do
with my past, particularly my deep-seated insecurities from childhood, and
with my general intolerance of ambiguity. We've learnt a lot about how
past and present structures interact for the individual, through thinking
about the formal similarities in the parental and present situations, and the
way feelings emerge even when the intention of the present structure is
entirely different from the past ones in which the feeling originally
emerged.

For example, the worry about not knowing. This is a real question
as to how to relate to another sexual relationship without being part of it,
and yet affecting it and being affected by it. Elsewhere, I mentioned how,
when Pete and Mary started sleeping together I kept on dreaming about
them as my parents. Well, in my family situation, as a child, there didn't
seem to be any sex going on between my parents, and, in fact, they slept
in different rooms, with my room in between their rooms. They each
seemed to have more of an emotional relationship with me that with each
other and each colluded with me against the other. The only occasions
when they were closer to each other than to me was when they were
colluding together against me. I knew they were planning something
against me if I was excluded from their goings on, and they were. Usually
it was to send me to hospital to have my tonsils out without telling me
beforehand, or planning who they would dump me with when they went
on holiday. I never learnt to handle a situation where I was excluded but
where nothing was being done against me, because this never was the case,
or so it seemed. Most children probably learn this because their parents are
together in the same bed every night, but mine never were. Also I was an
only child so I never had to relate to close relationships between others

(siblings and parents), which weren't against me.

So in a way, the real problems of the present structure inter-mingle with my childhood memories of exclusion and lead to paranoid thoughts quite at odds with what we all intend. Maybe it means that for the first time I am having to come to terms with a close relationship which I'm not directly involved in. Anyway, understanding that my experience of it includes elements quite separate from the real worries, makes them easier to cope with at the time, and makes me less worried about "feeling jealous". My past situation doesn't determine my reaction to the present one, which is in no sense a replica, but my past fed into it at the level of feelings.

Another example, which I think explains the other aspect of my jealousy, shows how the structure and the way we have worked things out, creates situations and differences between us, for which there is no immediate or spontaneous counterpart in the past. Working out a sexual relationship with Pete is not a symmetrical thing for him and me: for me, it is really the first time I have been able to express myself closely to any-one sexually, and to break down the barrier between affection and sex. For him, though, working out another sexual relation, this wasn't the case. So in a sense my sexual identity is very much more tied up with him, and the character of my sexuality, insofar as there isn't any innate sexuality, is very much more tied up with him as the only person I am sexually involved with at present. But for him, his sexual identity is tied up with two of us, not just with me, and it sometimes seems very paradoxical that the things that he and I have worked out bear a different relation to each of us."

CRITIQUE
OF THE THEORY
AND PRACTICE
OF PSYCHOANALYSIS

THE SOCIAL CONTEXT

In the previous section, we tried to show how our theory related to our practice, our attempts to act in a political manner through analysing the contradictions within our own relations and thinking about how we could relate that to an analysis of capitalist personal relationships and the family. We argued that theorising about anything means confronting the issues of the relation between theory and mass practice; of the current divide between the theory of an educated elite and the untheoretical consciousness of the working class; of the divide between theory and our lived experience. The social conditions for developing theory depend on facing these issues. The kind of theory a theory is, depends on the kind of social conditions, the kind of practical relation it has to the social reality within which it is produced.

In this part of the pamphlet, we want to analyse a theory of sexuality, Freud's, for the kind of theory it is, and its practical relation to the social reality of capitalism. The reason for doing this is not to have an intellectual debate with Freud. The reason is rather that we think that Freudian theory represents, in a transformed version, many of the assumptions that are built into the lived experience of capitalist sexual relations: there is a definite relation between the ideological consciousness, the ways we think and feel capitalist sexual relations when within them, and the ideological theory which we think Freudian theory is. So this is the first political point in analysing Freud, to trace out the relation between Freudian theory and everyday consciousness within capitalist sexual relations (we are not concerned with the way Freudian theory has slipped into 'common sense', so much as how common sense was open to assimilating Freudian theory in the first place, in a two-way traffic between ideological theory and consciousness).

The second political point is that in analysing the social conditions under which Freudian theory was produced, and its relation between theory and practice, we want to emphasise that we all do our thinking under social conditions not chosen by us and we are affected by them: primarily the capitalist division of labour and a hierarchically selective education system reproducing it. We all struggle in a conflict between what we take to be one basis for knowledge, our lived experience which is untheoretical, and theory, which tends to be academic, acquired in a study group or some way that differs little from the kind of study found in a university except for the texts it chooses to read, which often does not help us to theorise our own practice. So an analysis of Freud will aim to show the social conditions under which we all do our thinking, to point to the political problem of changing those conditions. The most revolutionary text can be treated in an academic way, nullifying any revolutionary meaning.

With the gulf between experience and theory, it is often difficult to treat any theory, let alone work out new theory or write pamphlets, except in the way we have been educated to, academically. But some theory, theory which is related to capitalist social reality in a passive way, not to any possibility of a mass practice to change it, actually reinforces the split between elitist theory and the untheoretical, passive experience of the lived relations of capitalism. Such a theory, we think, is Freud's. (Reich did try to link a theory of sexuality with a mass practice of changing sexuality. But because he borrowed many of his deepest assumptions from Freud, and saw the problem as one of liberating instinctual biological sex from social repression, and not one of social sexual relations with definite historical forms, we think it more direct to look at those assumptions and understand how they came to be thought in the first place.)

We shall give an outline of Freudian theory. Then we shall show how his ideas are related to capitalist social relations and their everyday consciousness. Finally we shall try to show that this relation between the theory of sexuality and capitalist reality is based on the social conditions of production of his theory: the relation between his theory, his practice and that reality. But before doing this, some general points about the social context of psychoanalysis.

Psychoanalysis is not only a body of concepts, a theoretical system. It is also a therapeutic method. It is also based on a particular methodology, a technical practice. It is also a widespread social institution in Western capitalist countries, and implies a particular social way of treating those designated (by themselves or others) as in need of treatment, as mad-neurotic-psychotic. As a form of treatment, psychoanalysis aims to cure those who have deviated from normal sexual development: it acts as a regulator within the context of what counts as normal for the rest of society, as well as being a theory of what is normal. It is not linked to a practice which aims to change the 'normality' of capitalist sexual development, of capitalist sexual relations.

Psychoanalysis involves professional training for analysts, which includes being analysed oneself, but above all this means that it is a profession exercised by a highly specialised group in the social division of labour (not to speak of high pay). As a consequence, those directly experiencing psychoanalysis are a tiny minority of the population. Granted that psychoanalysis is performed by an expert, and so relies on a highly selective educational system, it could only ever be of use to a tiny few, since it requires an intensive and lengthy relationship between therapist and patient.

This list of some of the different aspects of psychoanalysis does not in any way say what the relationship is between them. We shall try to analyse that. But whatever the relationship is, we don't think that it is possible simply to take the theory, think this or that aspect of it is good — or more pretentiously, and with less grounds, is scientific — and ignore all the other aspects of the practical relation the theory has to the social reality, including in particular its methodological practice. To take the theory as a system of concepts, and forget or discard the rest, is the academic relation to theory, the way we have been taught to relate to theory as an abstract body of ideas throughout our education.

While leaving till later a more detailed account of the relation between theory and practice in psychoanalysis, it's worthwhile saying a few global things about it. The theory developed along with changes in the way patients were being treated in mental hospitals, changes in therapeutic methodology. These changes, by producing different effects on patients than the old methods, produced completely different kinds of evidence, transformed the reality that was being theorised. Before, the methods had been ones like water therapy (bathing was seen as soothing agitated nerves), chemical methods, electric shock (it goes back that far, to the beginning of the century). Freud had used all these methods. But he made a break with them first by the use of hypnosis, and then by the use of what came to be psychoanalysis proper: the use of dream analysis and free association — speaking without reservation or self-censorship whatever comes into your mind.

The first change, the use of hypnosis, is perhaps the more crucial historical break with the past. For it changed the treatment of 'madness' from being a medical treatment by physical means (as all the old methods were), into being a psychological or mental treatment, a treatment using a special state of mind of the patient — hypnosis — not induced by physical means. This change is a crucial one. It meant that madness could be theorised not as a purely physiological or moral phenomenon. Madness became thought of as psychological. A theory of mental forces was connected with the new practice, hypnosis, a practice of acting on the patient's thoughts. You can trace the shift in theory in Freud's earliest writings.

But the change was only a partial one. It had come out of a medical practice, which like the treatment of physical diseases, treated individuals as the bearers of the disease, this time a mental disease or disorder. As such the practice was still linked to acting on each individual taken separately. There was no sense of there being social causes which had to be acted on by social and political means. Madness was seen as psychological, as something disordered within the individual, not as a disorder or contradiction in social relations. This was closely connected to the fact that hypnosis acted only on the mind of the individual being treated.

As an example of the way the practice was related to the theory, it's worth pointing out that it was through hypnosis that the theory of the unconscious first arose, a theory which has been a cornerstone of Freudianism. The patient is put under hypnosis. This transforms the normal everyday consciousness of the patient. This shows in the way that the therapist can act on the patient's consciousness in a way quite different from normal conversation. In particular he can ask the patient to reveal memories of the past which the patient was unable to recall in normal waking consciousness, often memories significantly related to the onset of the 'disorder'. This led directly to the theory of there being an unconscious, ideas that were too painful to recall. The idea of an unconscious was further reinforced by the fact that the therapist could suggest to the patient that he do something, without being conscious of why, after emerging from hypnosis (post-hypnotic suggestion). The patient did so, and so demonstrated that people's behaviour can be governed by ideas of which they are not in the least conscious. The theory of the individual unconscious was therefore very directly related to this practical relation between the therapist and the individual patient. As such it reproduces one important aspect which was present in medical treatment.

We'll go into the way in which changes in the theory of psychoanalysis were related to the development of the classical technique of analysis in the last section. Here we'll just say a few more things about the psychoanalytical situation, which like the therapeutic relation to the individual patient, constitutes its general social characteristics.

In psychoanalysis, the patient lies on the couch, and apart from recounting dreams, says whatever comes into his head, following the often illogical associations between one thing and another. The therapist interprets, mostly in common sense terms, what the patient says, to the patient. This interpretation principally takes the form of indicating links between the different, apparently disconnected succession of thoughts. It does not involve the therapist giving the patient a theoretical account of himself. It is not a joint process in which patient and therapist are together developing theory on an equal basis. The patient does not acquire theory through being analysed; (he can of course read up about it outside, but that is another matter not integral to the analytical situation).

On the other hand, the psychoanalyst does have a theory of what is going on, which, to varying degrees he keeps from the patient. It is through the interaction between therapist and patient that the therapist does develop his theory, not only about each individual patient, but a general theory. So, there is a divide between the consciousness of the patient, including the way it changes during the course of the treatment, and the theory of the therapist. The psychoanalyst is the trained expert in understanding. The patient is only the understood: the real changes in self-understanding that come to the patient from his analysis is not the route to being the expert, which requires further training, often medical training. An unequal division of knowledge is built into the psychoanalytical situation.

An expression of this unequal division of knowledge is the fact that the patient produces the raw material from his consciousness to be interpreted by the expert, while the psychoanalyst reveals nothing of himself for the patient to understand or interpret. Only accounts of experience come from one direction, only interpretations come from the other. After all it is the patient, the poor disordered individual, who is in need of care. We will indicate later that this peculiar form of human interaction is the basis of very specific concepts within psychoanalytical theory. Here, however, it is important to note that the practice of psychoanalysis reproduces another aspect of the medical relation between the expert and the patient: one person is the person who knows and acts on the basis of this knowledge, without the other person knowing what the basis is. The women's movement has discovered, even with physical diseases, that this inequality of knowledge is something which can itself be detrimental, particularly when most medical researchers and doctors are men.

But in the case of a theory about sexuality or about something which is 'mental', the problem is more acute. For, to accept this situation is to accept that there are experts in understanding and the rest who are just understood, when that understanding concerns the very fabric of all social relations we live everyday. This is built into the psychoanalytical situation, not just as an external condition. And it is closely related to the whole way in which it is the individual which is being understood. If there were a general social attempt to overcome the division between the expert and mass consciousness, it would immediately be a question of how the theory could be related to some collective social practice, or how the self-understanding of the working class could become theoretical.

But it is clear that in reproducing the medical relation to the individual patient, (or at most small group), psychoanalysis does in no way attempt to transform the everyday consciousness of the working class. Rather it picks off individual, mostly middle class, 'deviants' for special treatment. Its theory is related to that reality; not to the reality or practice of changing capitalism in a collective social practice. This is a crude point. But it is a defining context within which psychoanalysis operates. It defines the way in which the theory and practice of psychoanalysis relates to the overall social context within which it exists, and within which it creates the special 'phenomena of the couch' about which the theory is made.

The relation between the theory of the expert and the consciousness of the patient only reproduces what is a very general social division between the educated elite and the working class consciousness. The social division is one that is created in the first instance by a division between mental and manual labour, and the whole hierarchical educational system. Now, whether we like it or not, whether we challenge it or not, this is the context in which we all do our theorising — or not, depending on how high up the education system we got. The point is that psychoanalytical practice does not challenge it. It confirms it. What occurs in the therapeutic situation is only one particular instance of it. Even this is reflected directly in Freud's theory, as we shall see.

For, Freud does have a theory of how some things can be made conscious which were previously unconscious. But he has no theory of how consciousness can be transformed into theoretical consciousness. There is a complete dichotomy between his having a theory of consciousness and the consciousness which he theorises about, with no way to get to the former from the latter. This discontinuity only reflects the built-in division between the expert and the self-understanding of the patient on the couch. Freud's psychological theory of consciousness, based on the isolated individual on the couch, could never account for that social divide between theorist and theorised, a division created outside the consulting room, but inevitably present within it. Let alone provide a theory for developing a theoretical class consciousness to overcome that divide.

AN OUTLINE OF FREUDIAN THEORY

In this section, we outline the main aspects of Freud's theory of mental processes in general and sexuality in particular. There isn't space to give much sense of how Freud argues or presents the evidence for his theory. But we have presented his concepts as he saw them fitting together, showing how the specific theories and concepts rest on and are elaborations of, his more general and basic assumptions. So in this section we have tried to be faithful to Freud's own conception of his theory, though obviously as we understand it. Only in following sections will we step outside Freud's framework to criticise his theory for the way it reflects and reinforces everyday capitalist consciousness.

Instincts and the external world

The separation of the individual and the external world

One of Freud's most basic assumptions is that the individual is a system with its own laws of operation independent of, though interacting with, the external world. He was a physiologist before he was a psychologist, and he took it for granted that the individual as a psychological entity could be thought of in the same way as an individual biological organism. Looked at as a biological organism, an animal or human being could be thought of as a physical system which has to interact with the external world in order to survive (e.g. by getting and digesting food), but which it does with a specific physical apparatus of its own (muscles, sense organs, digestive system) with its own principles of operation. Whatever the particular features of an organism's environment, these processes have their own way of operating, depending on the species. Of course, differences in the environment, such as the availability of food, will affect how the organism develops in size, in health; but all these are minor modifications to the development of an organism (leaving out here the question of evolution — we're talking about the interaction between the individual organism and the environment, not the very different level of species interaction). All human foetuses have the same kind of physical apparatus: when and where they are born will affect styles and quantities of food, etc. But looked at as a biological organism, the same principles of operation would apply to a stone age child as to a child of 20th century capitalism.

This is a model which enables you to study the organism relatively separately from studying the external world. At the very least, there is a level of the organism's operation that can be studied independently of its interaction with the external world. There is no need to characterise with independent concepts the external world as part of a theory explaining how the organism operates internally.

Freud's view of the mental apparatus is analogous to this model. There are basic processes that characterise the mental aspect of the organism's system. Although vast differences in mental development and behaviour occur owing to individuals' interactions with the external world, the way the interactions affect the mind is bounded by the nature of the mental processes themselves. Therefore it is possible to study the individual mind as a relatively separate system. The external world is seen by Freud as a series of obstacles to the individual, which though they may be systematic, are not conceptualised as such, and so have the status of 'accidental' events which may befall the individual.

This is all to say that Freud takes into his psychology the universalism and ahistoricism of the biological model. This carries into his sociology as well: there is no independent characterisation of society (the world external to the psychological individual), no specific laws of social development, so society is a universal and unhistorical concept. These aspects of Freud's theory are a consequence of the radical separation he makes between the individual and the external world, the subject and the object, which is what these opening remarks have tried to explain.

The nature of mental processes

We have seen that Freud's conception of the psychological individual is analogous to a biological conception of an individual organism. But biology is much more intimately part of his theory of mental processes than mere analogy, as we shall see from his concept of instinct.

The concept of instinct is one which stands between the biological and the psychological. Taking again the simple example of eating: the organic need for food causes chemical and muscular activity in the stomach, which is an internal stimulation felt by the hungry organism. Feeling hungry isn't pleasurable, so it leads to action to end the stimulation — getting food. Now, the instinct isn't just the activity of the stomach or the feeling that leads to eating, but the two together. Instincts are the biological basis for the activities animals must perform in order to keep themselves alive. Therefore there are instinctual bases of sex too: stimulation arising from the genitals (in many animals it is periodic 'heat', the result of seasonal physiological changes) is felt as tension that can be reduced by sexual activity.

Though instincts are the basis of the individual and species survival activities, there are not inbuilt patterns of action, necessarily. It is important to be clear on this; while holding a strong theory of instincts, Freud, like much of later psychology, does not think people's behaviour is innate. Freud thinks that instinct-based activities such as getting food or sex (which he calls the aim of instincts), and the kinds of food or the kinds of people or things sexually aimed at, (which he calls the objects of instincts), are not given in the instincts, but are developed through the infant's interactions with the external world.

What is given is the mental energy which arises from the various bodily sources, and which has immutable properties of its own. The overall aim of the mental apparatus is to reduce the level of tension caused by energy that is not discharged in the appropriate satisfaction of the instinct. Instinctual energy appears in consciousness as feelings of pain or pleasure: pain or tension is felt when the energy is pressing to be released; pleasure is the feeling of release. So the fundamental principle of operation of the mental processes is the pleasure principle, based on the nature of the instincts. Towards the end of his life, Freud attempted to explain the existence of the pleasure principle, itself a feature of instincts, as arising from a fundamental instinct of all organic life: the aim to return to a state of rest. On the basis of biological speculation, each individual organism's development was viewed as development towards its own natural death, survival activity being aimed at preventing death from external causes; that is to say, towards a state of lifeless inorganic inactivity. He called this the death instinct. It subsumed the pleasure principle, since it explained the aim towards reduction of tension.

The theory of the death instinct may make Freud's theory of instincts sound very metaphysical and teleological; but as he uses the concept it is much less global in his theory than has been suggested here. Let us look more closely at what he says of the sexual instinct. Although Freud speaks of the sexual instinct, he is being more precise when he talks of the sexual instincts. He thinks there are initially a number of sexual instincts which only gradually integrate with each other to form the basis of adult sexual activity. As we have said, an instinct is a source of mental energy arising from a bodily organ. Some parts of the body give rise to a particular kind of mental energy called libido, which finds its release in sensuous activities with the parts of the body that give rise to it. These specia¹ parts of the body can be the site of physical pleasure for its own sake, as distinct from pleasure connected with the fulfilment of some other physical need like eating, and are called erotogenic zones. The mental energy arising from them is sexual energy, libido. The sexual instincts, therefore, are the internal stimulations and feelings connected with various parts of the body, that lead a child to look for some kind of sensuous contact with those parts of the body. These are the component ₁nstincts of the sexual instinct, each starting off with a different specific aim and a different object, but associated under the same name by virtue of their aims all being sensuous.

Sexual development in infancy is a process whereby one after another the erotogenic zones become active, and are gradually connected with things and people outside the infant's own body. The first erotogenic zone to be stimulated is the mouth in feeding; and the first activity the child discovers sensuous pleasure in is sucking. So the first sexual aim is sucking. The child, sucking its thumb, is taking itself as its first sexual object: children are initially autoerotic − giving sensuous pleasure to themselves, including masturbation a little later on. The anus is the next erotogenic zone to become active. This idea of there being states, oral then anal, is not seen by Freud as a laid-down pattern of infantile development determined by natural causes within. Rather, it follows the pattern of interaction with the external world that is an inevitable consequence of just the general growth of the child: at the newborn stage the main interaction the baby has with the external world is being fed. As the muscles develop, toilet training becomes possible, and so the anus can become the focus of attention. As the child becomes more adept and exploratory, and can use its hands more, the genitals are more likely to be discovered as a source of sensuous pleasure, for girls the clitoris, for boys the penis.

As the child discovers the pleasures of its own body, at the same time other people are becoming the object of affection through the caring relations they have to the child. Infantile sexual development includes the harnessing of the child's developing sensuous aims to their affectionate impulses for people as sexual objects.

Full adult sexuality only develops after puberty, when the sexual instinct arising from the genitals gets stronger. Freud sees this strengthening of the genitals over the other erotogenic zones partly as a result of adolescent physical development. But really he doesn't see the eventual predominance of the genitals as a natural feature of the sexual instincts. The other sexual component instincts continue to exist, and he begins to talk of genital sexuality as something to be achieved, not something given. We have to qualify the definition of sexual instincts given earlier as having a sensuous aim which is only the attainment of sensuous pleasure. Freud actually had an additional conception of what counted as sexual: those activities which are directed towards the end of reproduction. This is a biological aim, and requires that the various elements of the sexual instinct are all eventually united under the dominance of the genital instinct. Anal and oral sex should only have the status of foreplay, not be the main sexual aims. But his biological aim of reproduction is guaranteed by the nature of the sexual instincts themselves. So, customs, restrictions, taboos, have to play a part in ensuring it, and to guide the choice of sexual object. For, genital sex is only able to fulfil the biological aim if the object is a whole person, a person of the opposite sex, and a person to whom affection as well as sensuous aims is directed, since reproduction includes the childrearing couple. The determination of object choice will be further explained below.

It should now be clearer how the instincts in Freud's conception are both a fundamental force in determining human activity, and do not ensure any specific content of that activity. Freud radically separates the source of sexual and other instinctual energy within the individual from its aims and objects. It is this basic conception that enables him to make a coherent theory of instincts which also allows for both the enormous variation in human sexual behaviour and the existence of a norm or biological aim of sexuality. To see exactly how he sees this working, we shall have to look a bit more closely at the sort of things mental energy from instincts can do, that enables it to be expressed in so many different ways.

At the beginning, the energy arising from the instincts has only an 'economic' aim, to be reduced in quantity through being released. It can attach itself very freely to different ideas, images, and things, and is very mobile. For example, the mother's breast, a source of milk, can become itself an image that satisfies the child, in its own right, because of its association with the satisfaction of being fed. Even the hallucinated image instead of the real thing can excite the child, and be a focus of libido. This mobility of energy is described by Freud in terms of two principles of operation: displacement and condensation. Displacement is the process whereby energy moves from one idea or thing to another. Condensation is the process whereby a single thing or idea can come to be the focus of several different currents of instinctual energy. These primary mental processes mean that it is a long term process of development of the mental apparatus before any attachment of instinct, object and aim is stabilised.

There are two kinds of transformations that instincts can spontaneously undergo, that will be important to know about when we come to talk about variations of sexual development later on. Freud calls these 'conversion of an active into a passive aim', or vice versa; and 'turning of an instinct back on the subject'. An example of the first would be the conversion of the sexual aim of touching into being touched; looking into being looked at: the sexual release initially obtained actively now being fully satisfied passively. Here, an 'active' aim doesn't necessarily mean more mental energy to achieve its end: it might mean more exertion and ingenuity to get looked at than to look. An example of the second type of transformation would be for the aim of touching another person to be turned into the aim to touch oneself. Here it is not the aim that has ceased to be active, but the aim has turned away from the external object back onto the subject.

These transformations are not treated by Freud as just descriptive of different kinds of sexual behaviour. On the contrary, he ascribes them to basic inbuilt features of instinctual processes. A great deal of his theory rests on these initial concepts, as does his theory of culture, as expressions of the basic mental processes.

The interaction of the individual with the external world

The organised and complex mind of an adult individual develops through the interaction between the primary processes described above, and the external world. The primary processes of the mind act on the pleasure principle, press for immediate release, and roam freely over any objects and aims which can allow this release. But the kinds of action needed to survive in the world have to be more organised, consistent and planned. This is in conflict inevitably with the immediacy and mobility of the primary mental processes. Out of this conflict, between instinctual activity and the external world, Freud constructs the idea of a basic, developing, conflict inside the individual, a conflict between two types of instinct, the sexual instinct and the self-preservative instinct, as we shall now see.

When the infant is first born, all its physical needs are satisfied without any effort on its own part: being fed and held (its needs for survival) coincide with the satisfaction of its sensuous aims. As the child grows, some things aren't immediately available any more. As its horizons widen, the child wants things it can't have or can't have without effort or planning. Some wants are incompatible with others, or have to be delayed. So the original principle of mental functioning, the pleasure principle, has to be modified by what Freud calls the reality principle. The mental functioning which gradually develops to cope with these conflicts are thought and perception. The particular quality of the external world becomes more important to the child. Its sense organs develop, attention and memory develop, all processes necessary to act instrumentally on the world. Consciousness is a secondary aspect of mental processes, that emerges as a result of the conflict between the pleasure principle and the reality principle.

The reality principle is only a modification of the pleasure principle. It's there to guarantee a greater balance of pleasure over pain in the long run. But also, the reality principle involves a real struggle against the pleasure principle. The kind of pleasure that is incompatible with the reality principle is sensuous pleasure. For a little infant, there is no way that sexuality could be developed according to the reality principle, because the child has no properly developed sexual organs and responses. In other aspects of education, there can be an education of an instinct, moulding it into a realistic pattern of activity — learning to eat only at meal times. But for the sexual instincts, they are just overridden by the education of these other, self-preservative instincts, because, according to Freud, there is no basis for a moderate expression of sexuality in infancy. The struggle against infantile sexuality is waged with the energy that comes from the self-preservative instinct. It is a struggle that goes on within the individual, and results in a new form of organisation of the mind. A special agency differentiates itself out, with the two special tasks of organising instrumental activity towards the world, and of chaining the sexual impulses that would threaten to interfere with that. This agency is called the Ego. Because both its tasks are aimed to express the self-preservative instincts as against the sexual instincts, the self-preservative instincts are also called ego-instincts.

The nature of the difference between sexual and ego-instincts is not made very clear by Freud, and he revised the theory more than once. He thought they were probably qualitatively different kinds of energy at one time; and at another that there was just a functional difference in the way energy was deployed once it reached the mental apparatus. Anyway these details are not important here. What is, is that Freud thought that certain types of neurosis in adults could be explained by the blockage of sexual impulses in infancy in a way that did not let them have any expression except as transformed energy, discharged in neurotic symptoms. The initial blockage arose from a conflict with the external world. In the process, a contradiction was set up inside the individual between the two instincts, a conflict mediated by the ego. Freud's view of the initial, natural and inevitable antagonism and interaction between the instinctual individual and the external world, leads to a theory of the development of contradictions within the mental organisation of the individual.

Consciousness and unconsciousness

The development of consciousness and unconsciousness

The story of the development of the ego is the story of the development of consciousness and unconsciousness. The ego's first task of directing activity towards the external world involves the emergence of consciousness, a specific part of the mind able to monitor the external world. And the ego's second task, the blocking of the direct expression of sexuality, involves the dynamic activity of putting sexual ideas and impulses out of consciousness, and keeping them in a specific mental state of unconsciousness. Originally, all mental processes are unconscious. The development of the ego creates a dynamic unconsciousness, that could only arise once consciousness had begun to emerge. A dynamic unconscious means a mental state that requires constant energy to keep things unconscious. Unconscious impulses are pressing for expression in consciousness, activity. The activity of the ego which prevents this is called repression. So consciousness and unconsciousness develop in active relation to each other, a relation mediated by the ego.

What is it that is repressed, made unconscious? So far we have said that it is the energy arising from the sexual instinct. We have also explained how the sexual energy or libido is very mobile, changing objects and aims. Sexual objects and aims are chosen via consciousness: they involve the external world. And the external world for the child is its immediate family, parents, brothers and sisters. What is repressed, therefore, is not instinctual energy as such, but the specific sexual wishes directed towards the parents. It doesn't make sense to speak of the instinct itself being repressed, because instincts are partly physiological anyway. Their energy can only become mental in the form of some idea, picture, image, word. When sexual instinct is directed as a sexual wish (say, to kiss or be beaten) towards a particular person, say the father, then Freud calls that a desire, a crucial Freudian concept. It is desires, wishes towards particular people, that are subject to repression, not just free-floating sexual instincts.

The desires of a child for its parents do not involve only sensuous wishes, but also emotions of love and hate. As the child grows, affection and emotional attachments come out of the dependence of the child on the parents for food and other care. Both the affectionate and sensuous currents are satisfied by the same person – to begin with the mother. Gradually the child's sensuous and affectionate impulses become fused together in relation to her. This is the child's first love relationship. It is the obstacles that a boy or girl encounters in expressing this first love relationship that lead up to the major act of repression in childhood, determining the nature of the unconscious desires the child carries into adulthood. This first love relationship, and the connected feelings it arouses towards the other parent, and brothers and sisters, is called the Oedipus Complex. It is a momentous phase in the development of the relation between consciousness and unconsciousness.

Freud's theory of the Oedipus Complex changed over time. To begin with, it was based on his analysis of himself, and was a picture of the development of a boy-child. The boy's first sexual love for his mother makes him a rival and hostile to his father. He would like to oust his father as his mother's lover (as King Oedipus did). At first Freud just extrapolated the Oedipus complex for girls as being symmetrical. He assumed that her first love was the father, with hostility to the mother. This obviously involves a crude idea about the natural mutual attraction of opposite sexes.

The complex of feelings towards parents, blossoming by the fourth year or so, meets obstacles — neither love nor hate can be safely expressed. These obstacles include the child's own genital inadequacies to express full sexual love to the mother. But the main ones are the parents' prohibitions and punishments of the child's sexuality. These threats arouse the castration complex. The castration complex is a fear that the father will punish the boy by castration, for his rivalry and possessive love for the mother and for his aggressive feelings towards the father. The particular fear for his penis comes from the fact that his love for the mother is partly composed of strictly sexual feelings by now; and is fed by his having by now seen that women, maybe his sister, do not have a penis, which he concludes is because they have lost it. The result of these fears and threats is that in the interests of self-protection, by an act of repression carried out by the ego, the boy gives up the whole set of feelings of the Oedipus complex, and replaces them in consciousness by more acceptable ones: sexless affection for the mother and affectionate identification with the father. The sexual feelings and ideas are completely repressed in later years, until puberty.

Later on Freud realised that the girl's first love object is also her mother, and she feels hostile to her father. Her castration complex consists in feeling she has already been castrated, and her turning away from her original love object is connected with disappointment in discovering her mother's castration, and realising that she can only get a penis (baby) from the father. She abandons the sexual aim of her love when she realises the inferiority of her clitoris, and so stops masturbating, repressing all her sexual impulses until puberty.

Having crudely outlined the Oedipus complex in its simplest form, we should now explain how its repression by the ego affects the development of consciousness and unconsciousness. Hostility towards the father and love for the mother are feelings that are not in accordance with the reality principle of the ego-instincts: the child feels himself to be endangered by them. The ego, operating for self-preservation, pushes these feelings for the parents out of consciousness, and at the same time constructs conscious feelings to replace them. These different conscious feelings act as the ego's defenses against the repressed but still active impulses and thoughts. The boy's (we'll say more about girls later) hostility to the father is turned into affection. That is to say, the instinctual energy that fed the hatred is mobilised to a different, and transformed, aim. This attraction of energy to an opposite idea in consciousness (affection) from the idea to which it is attached in unconsciousness (hostility), is called reaction formation. It is one of the main mechanisms of defence of the ego.

At the same time as substituting affection for hostility, the ego takes into itself the father's prohibition on sex with the mother, which was the initial cause of the hostility. The external prohibition becomes an internal taboo. Part of the ego is separated out and set up as a source of rules, standards and ideals which originally came from without. This part of the ego is called the super-ego. It is an unconscious part of the ego, which is felt consciously only as conscience and guilt. This means that the child now has internally constructed inhibitions against his own sexuality. The emotional power of these inhibitions and ideals, like the incest taboo, comes from their dynamic relation to the original sexual feelings, now repressed. The joint process whereby hostility is turned into affection, and prohibitions into internal rules, is called identification. It is said that the Oedipus Complex is dealt with in the boy by his identification with the father. This word has the more commonsense force of 'identification' meaning 'wanting to be like the father' or 'thinking you are like the father', as well as signalling the ego's processes, because it is the process whereby the boy is able to take a masculine course of future development, since the father is now an internalised ideal for him.

This is how the Oedipus complex is supposed ideally to be resolved. The ego should be able to use the energy attached to the unconscious ideas, to develop alternative conscious ideas and feelings, not only of a sexual kind, but also to fuel intellectual and practical activities. Sublimation is the name given to this successful rechannelling of the energy of repressed desire. But usually the process isn't complete, and some of the energy remains attached to the unconscious desires. This is called fixation of the libido. When this happens, the desires cannot change or dispel, but remain active inside the individual, always pressing to be expressed somehow. They can't express themselves directly and explicitly, and so attach themselves to other ideas and feelings which are sufficiently unlike the original in appearance to be acceptable to the ego. For example, a neurotic symptom of hysterical coughing, which appears unsexual, could be the expression of an unconscious desire for oral sex with the father. The ego 'compromises' and allows a very roundabout discharge of libido — in a cough.

Where there is a fixation of an unconscious infantile desire, a large part of a person's behaviour will consist of this kind of roundabout behaviour. This is especially true of a person's love relations. The choice of a love object may look like the opposite of the original. A man who is fixated unconsciously at the childhood desire for his mother may choose only boys to love. The real dynamic and content of what happens in his relationships comes from the particular pattern of feeling that was repressed but still urges to be acted out. But he is unconscious of this, so that there is a sense in conscious love relationships that they are compulsive and beyond the individual's control. Relationships based on unconscious desire are called phantasy relationships, because their basis is not present reality but past unconscious desire.

The relation between consciousness and unconsciousness

There are two aspects to Freud's conception of the relation between conscious and unconscious parts of the mind: there is a relationship of meaning and a relationship of energy dynamics. Both of these have to be understood in order to understand his theory of cure, which consists partly in 'becoming conscious of what is unconscious'. The meaning relation. Conscious thought and behaviour of all kinds – dreams, jokes, ways of acting in love, neurotic symptoms – seemed to Freud to be gappy, obscure, contradictory, and only comprehensible by postulating another level of the mental processes, a kind of deep structure that gave meaning and coherence to the appearances on the surface.

The dream was the first example Freud explored in depth, and it became the prototype of the meaning relation between consciousness and unconsciousness. In sleep, the ego's defences relax enough to allow the emergence of unconscious desires. A dream is an enactment in phantasy of the unconscious desire, a wish-fulfillment. As such dreams are formed in accordance with the mode of operation of the unconscious – the primary processes we explained earlier of displacement and condensation. So a dream image can stand for something else: a purse can be a vagina. The link is that they both have something in common, say, as containers. This creates a verbal or visual connection between them. In the unconscious, energy is transferred by such associative connections, often quite arbitrary ones. So part of the dream is due to the character of the unconscious. However, in the interests of the ego's defences, the unconscious desire has to be disguised, and attached to a different content. The events of the previous day are used as the material out of which the ego fashions ideas which disguise the dream's wish. So a dream is a compromise formation which has to be translated into the language of the unconscious to be understood.

Symptoms are another compromise formation. They too are under partial control of the unconscious. They show features of the primary processes too: a single act, like an obsessional ritual such as hand washing, could stand for several unconscious desires. A symptom is a huge condensation of meaning into a single action, as a dream can be a condensation of many complex meanings into a single image.

The energy relation. Because of the meaning relation, some commentators of Freud have been tempted to think of the relation between consciousness and unconsciousness as just two different levels of meaning, the same thing but with two sides, a single text which needed deciphering because written in a strange script: consciousness as the back of a tapestry, with the unconscious as the front with the real picture: the same stitches give a meaningless back and the coherent front. If this were all it was, psychoanalysis would only have to reveal to the patient the meaning of his experiences for him to be cured. Psychoanalysis would be just a method of interpretation.

But in fact, Freud is very clear that telling the patient the content of his unconscious desires is not a condition for cure. It is not equivalent to the process of becoming conscious of what is unconscious. This is because the conscious and the unconscious are two separate mental processes, separated and related by balances and transfers of energy. If an interpretation of the unconscious desire is given to the patient by the analyst, the situation then is that the idea exists in the patient's mind in two forms, as a conscious thought or piece of information; and as an unconscious idea attached to sexual energy, held dynamically out of consciousness by the mechanisms of the ego. Just knowing the idea does not in itself alter this dynamic. Becoming conscious is an emotional as well as an intellectual process, and involves altering the organisation of the mind, breaking down the ego's resistances by undoing repression. This is supposed to be achieved in psychoanalysis only through the patient's 'love' for the doctor. Analysis can only be successful if the patient transfers to the person of the doctor the unconscious desires for the parents which are at the root of the neurosis. This is called transference love. By thus activating the desire, but not permitting it to be expressed, the doctor has a way into dismantling the patient's resistances.

Once a patient is able to face the unconscious desires, the cure is finished. He is given the chance of freely deciding how to act, which he can't do so long as his desires are unconscious, and therefore compulsive.

Theory of sexuality

As we've said, Freud doesn't think there is a natural pattern of sexual behaviour for adults, laid down instinctively. Adult sexuality is constructed for each individual through interaction with the external world of people and bodies. But he does have an idea as to what is normal or ideal for adult sexuality. It is important to get clear what sort of normativeness this is — it isn't primarily ethical or evaluative, though it does have evaluative connotations. And it isn't statistical: most people don't fulfill it, so it isn't a norm in that sense. Freud sees sexual development as the achievement or failure at certain tasks, which most people more or less fail because these tasks are very complicated and there are many 'vicissitudes' that can befall an instinct in the course of its interactions with the world.

The tasks facing each individual are:

the uniting of the component sexual instincts under the primacy of the genitals;

the uniting of the sexual and affectionate currents of feeling, directing them towards the same object;

focussing the sexual and affectionate currents on a whole person of the opposite sex;

the investment of sexual energy in new sexual objects after puberty, not the first objects of desire the parents.

These tasks are posed by the biological aim of reproduction. As we said earlier, Freud thinks sex is for reproduction. This is one sense in which he has a normative idea of sexual development. We also said that he thinks sex might legitimately be defined as sensuous pleasure which has to be modified by the reproductive aim. And this is another way in which his normative ideas come in. If the infantile desires for the parent(s) are not renounced, the individual will become ill. This may take the form of severe and obvious neuroses; or the milder form of compulsive repetitions of painful love relations; or general ineffectiveness in the practical and intellectual tasks of life, owing to the blockage of energy that would fuel these activities. By 'ill' Freud means the individual will be subject to contradictory forces acting from within him, which may counter his conscious intentions, but over which he has no control. So we can now see why he has a normative idea of the 'tasks' facing each individual in his sexual development. Unless he fulfills them, he will not be as effective and instrumental a person as he might be, and he will be unhappy and frustrated.

Freud explains the various forms of adult sexuality and neuroses in terms of the different ways in which people deal with the tasks described above. To give some idea of how these explanations go, we will pick out four examples of important aspects of adult sexuality, and briefly say what Freud says about them. The four are: i) the development of female sexuality; ii) the split some people have between sexual and loving feelings; iii) homosexuality; iv) and two different patterns of feeling involved in 'being in love'.

Feminine sexuality   Here we can clearly see that Freud's idea of 'successful' feminine development is underlaid by his normative conception that sex is for biological reproduction, and that there are neurotic conflicts set up if the specific tasks necessary for this are not achieved.

Boys and girls both have an inborn bisexuality. Their sexual development is the same until the Oedipus complex, both in terms of sexual aims, (the oral, anal and genital stages, where the girl's genital is the clitoris), and in terms of objects (the self and then the mother). The Oedipus complex poses different and harder tasks for girls than for boys. While he has to abandon his love for his mother and his genital sexuality until puberty, when his genital sexuality is reawakened and directed towards another female which he loves; she, the girl-child, has to abandon her clitoral sexuality and her love for her mother, has to find an object of a different sex from this first love object, and in addition, has to transfer her centre of sexual excitement from the clitoris to the vagina.

Now, since the girl has to change more drastically in order to become 'feminine' than the boy has to to become 'masculine', Freud calls the early form of sexuality, common to both, masculine. It is characterised mainly by active aims and aggressive libidinal demands. Thus the tasks of the girl-child can be summarised as the task of overcoming her masculine impulses. This is precisely how Freud sees it. And he thinks that the process is such a complex and multi-staged one that it is likely to fail more or less, more often than not. The inbuilt bisexual tendency of everyone is one of the obstacles to the girl making the right choice: instead of abandoning her clitoral sexuality at the time of the Oedipus complex, she may cling to it, if there are strong masculine trends in her constitution. Or she may fail to turn the hostile rivalry with the father into affection, and instead may continue to resent him, not wanting to turn a wish for a penis into a wish for a penis-baby from him. This would be to maintain an active (destructive) aim towards him, instead of a passive one of wanting to be given something by him, which is the feminine aim conducive to reproduction.

Freud, therefore, doesn't see any natural development towards femininity. On the contrary, he thinks that if it were left to the impulses girls have received from nature, femininity would be unlikely to be achieved. The biological aim of reproduction is guaranteed not by the suitable development of both sexes, but by the characteristic sexuality of the male: his genital sexual desires are so urgent and masterful, and his early attachment to a love object of the opposite sex so strong, that his activity towards women is itself sufficient to ensure that the right kind of sex happens. The difficulties that women have to go through in making the right changes, are the cause of their being more neurotic women, according to Freud; also the cause of their being so much frigidity in women. He saw this as a sort of 'masculine protest' by women. It could either represent the continuation of the infantile desire for a woman as a love object, preventing her responding sexually to men; or her failure to change her centre of sexual excitement to the vagina; or it could be seen as revenge on the man for her father's rivalry for the mother.

The split between sex and affection   Some people, mostly men, according to Freud, find they can only have sex with a woman they don't have any other feeling for, and are more or less impotent with the woman they love. Freud explains this failure to fuse sex and affection as due to an unconscious fixation to the mother. His unconscious desire for her is disguised by his filial feelings of affection and respect. When he seeks sex with any other woman, it is his mother he is unconsciously seeking, but if affection were present too, this would bring him too close to the repressed and forbidden phantasy. So love and sex are split into two separate activities in his life, because they are split into different parts of his mind, conscious and unconscious.

Homosexuality   This has more than one explanation, because Freud thinks there are several routes to it. One of them, as an example, is the failure to re-attach sexual energy onto a new sexual object after the repression of the Oedipus complex. Instead, when he reaches adolescence, having lost his first object choice, the person will make himself the object of his libido, reverting to the autoerotic stage that existed even before the infantile relationship with the mother. This early stage is called primary narcissism, and the later form of object choice is called narcissistic. When a person does have relationships with other people, he will choose someone like himself, a person of his own sex, relating to himself through them.

Freud picks out two ways of being in love   Some people in love are dependent, clinging, lose their own identity in comparison with the loved one, idealise the qualities of the loved one, and feel inferior beside him/her. This is called anaclitic love (anaclitic means 'leaning on'), and it is the result of the continuing fixation at the stage of the child's first love relation with the parents, who cared for the child, and whom it 'leant upon' absolutely.

Other people are more interested in being loved that in loving in this idealising fashion. They choose people who reflect their own qualities, rather than feeling inferior to their lover. This is the result of the kind of object choice explained above as being narcissistic. Homosexuality is only one specific form of narcissistic love. Freud thinks narcissism is more characteristically feminine, because it has a more passive aim of being loved than loving. It is reflected in 'typical' feminine traits like vanity. But he concludes that in actual fact, both men and women are found who are narcissistic or anaclitic in their ways of being in love, or more usually, a bit of both, since none of these variations in sexual development described here are found in pure form.

Freud doesn't think these are special 'neurotic' forms of love. On the contrary, he thinks that compulsion, idealisation, etc, and the dominance of unconscious desire, are the essence of love. Love is a kind of neurosis, in the sense that it is underlain by some of the same mental processes, and often acts as a temporary resolution of neurosis.

A further task each individual has to achieve is to overcome the Oedipus complex in such a way as to allow energy to be released for activities other than sexual. When we say 'has to' be achieved, this means has to for culture and civilisation to develop. We can now see that this is the basis of Freud's normative ideas about the reasons for neurosis in sexual and feminine development: the kinds of sexual tasks channeling and repressing impulses, are needed not only for biological reproduction, but also for the reproduction of society. These tasks are therefore imposed by socialisation of children, which takes place against some biological characteristics of the individual, and so causes conflicts in individual development.

The processes which create civilisation are processes that happen within each individual. For example, Freud says quite a lot about the basis of intellectuality in individual development. A free and creative thinker will be someone whose earliest intellectual activities, which are the child's curiosity about where babies come from, are not completely repressed so leading to a sexual fixation of energy, but are freed to move about unrestrainedly. Many people are inefficient and limited because some of the energy involved in these early sexual researches is still unconsciously attached to them. Severe difficulties and blocks in thinking imaginatively would result from a violent and sudden infantile act of repression. As well as these routes to intellectuality via the fate of the sexual researches of infancy, different intellectual forms are associated with different neuroses. For example, there is a particular link between sex and thought in the kind of neurotic called obsessional. These people are suffering from an inability to express their sexuality in fully sexual forms: one of the defences the ego has against unconscious desires is thought itself, so the ego produces constant ideas and problems to think about to avoid the anxiety of repressed desires. So thought itself can be a neurotic symptom.

Other features of civilisation are social solidarity and altruism, which seem not to be individual features like intellectuality, but which are explained as such by Freud. Social solidarity has its basis in each separate individual making an act of identification with the others, on the basis of their sharing the same internal ideal of what they would like to be like. Altruism is an over-reaction to the guilt for the unconscious hostility to the father, with infantile roots. So the more people are kind and generous, the more they are individually split in the reaction of their conscious and their unconscious. Social and moral feelings and values arise out of infantile sexual repression, and so in their origin are really guilt and aggression.

We can now see how the theoretical separation Freud makes of the individual and the external world, has the paradoxical result that society comes to be explained by individual psychological processes. At the beginning of each individual life the interaction of the individual, with its own mode of operation, and the external world, leads to a complex restructuring of the organisation of the mind, setting up the dynamic relation between consciousness and unconsciousness. From then on, the individual's behaviour is primarily determined from within himself, by unconscious desire and the ego's defences against it. This dynamic between the unconscious and conscious inside each individual is what leads to social activities and interactions between individuals. Society therefore comes to be conceived as the outcome of interactions between these separate individual systems, each of which is determined by internal dynamic properties fundamentally and radically external to each other.

FREUDIAN THEORY
AND IDEOLOGICAL CONSCIOUSNESS

In this section, we are not simply opposing our ideas to Freud's as an alternative set of concepts. We are trying to show how Freud's theory is an ideology: that is to say is a reflection of the way capitalist relations are experienced from within them. It is not at all an obvious or direct reflection. Freud does have a theory that goes beyond, and often demystifies, common sense and the lived experience of the individual love, sex, thought, and so on. But nonetheless, his theoretical ideas have fundamentally the same assumptions as both common sense and untheoretical consciousness. His theory is thought within the framework of capitalist social relations, rather than explaining them. The capitalist reality of sexuality as we analysed it in the first pamphlet and here, is characterised by the dissociation, individualism, givenness and abstractness of feelings. Freud's theory reproduces these characteristics of capitalist reality in his theory. Where feelings are felt as given, Freud theorises as given, because governed by immutable principles of biological energy. Where feelings are felt as having their ultimate source within the individual, Freud theorises them as attributes of the individual's mental processes.

This is the kind of critique we are making of Freud's theory in this section. It cannot be made clear until it is made more concrete. So we will start with his theory of society and follow with his theory of sexuality.

Theory of society

Freud's theory of society has two aspects which intimately reflect capitalist reality. First, social processes are reduced to individual mental processes, and there is no independent theory of the social world external to the individual. Secondly, he reduces the whole range of social relationships to sexuality.

Reduction to individual processes

There are different strands in capitalist philosophy itself, but dominant ones share this feature of reductionism to the individual. One strand, laisser-faire liberalism, believes that society is a conglomerate of individuals each pursuing his own interests, and that this leads to the greater good of everyone. J.S.Mill, whom Freud admired, thought this worked quite benignly on the whole with the minimum of law and force; the less the better. Another strand is Hobbesian individualism. This has the same fundamental model of society as individuals pursuing their own interests, and the 'social' just being the result of their interactions. But he sees this as very fierce and aggressive, so that strong laws and force are necessary if these individuals are to hold together in society at all, rather than killing each other in pursuit of their own desires.

Freud's theory knocked the liberal faith in the benignity of individuals. He deeply shocked many contemporary liberals by his gloomy picture of the aggressive and egoistical basis of man's social and co-operative behaviour. But he retained the same social model as the liberals, basically in a Hobbesian form. The difference from Hobbes, which is really only a sophistication, was that the taboos and prohibitions on violence and complete selfishness are erected internally in each individual, not just imposed by strong laws. This is how he goes beyond liberalism. The internalisation of morality is his explanation of why the world can sometimes appear as the optimist liberals see it; there is no need for severe law if people have set up the constraints on their desires internally, and so act kindly and altruistically.

Now the reason why it is possible to theorise capitalist social processes as basically the effects of the interactions of individuals, is because that is precisely how the social workings of capitalism present themselves. Individualism is a social relation of capitalism. Capitalism structures ways of relating that construct people into individuals. There are a number of individualisms, intellectual, political, and emotional. Another is the wage relation, a social relation between capital and the individual wage worker — as if each individual made a separate contract with the capitalist, masking the collective and social character of the production process by socialising labour in a way distinctive to capitalism in the individual wage relation of many workers to the same capital.

Bourgeois philosophy emphasises that individuals are the sources of effective actions on the world. It is the epitome of the bourgeois ethic that change and construction come from strong and determined individuals (in the 19th century, men with an 'entrepreneurial' character). This is an ideology, because the only individuals whose actions on the world can be effective as individuals are those whom the capitalist social relations have put in a position of power. That is, the individual owners of the means of production (who increasingly no longer have even that marginal effectuality of individual action, owing to the development of monopoly capitalism, the large corporations). Their actions do not fundamentally have their source of effectiveness inside themselves, though, but in the particular social relations they are in, which enables their individual actions to have effect. The rest of the individuals in society, especially the working class, do not have the possibility of effective action as individuals, but only can change and construct things by collective action, which changes the social relations subordinating them, in an unequal power relation, to capital.

The idea that arises out of capitalist reality, that effectiveness of an individual's actions is due to the qualities of the individual, – how 'together' he is, how rational, how energetic, creative, imaginative – has entered deep into the heart of Freud's theory. Where intellectual individualism and the individualism of the active subject are part of the lived experience of capitalist reality, Freud explicitly theorises the effectiveness of thoughts and actions as being attributes of individuals. The ego is the agency which determines whether the individual shall act in accordance with reality, that is whether the individual shall be able to act instrumentally on the external world. Failures to achieve what an individual is aiming at are due to his ego's failures to properly mobilise libido away from unconscious sexual aims, so he remains under partially irrational control. Many of Freud's patients were professional men who found this was their problem.

This part of Freud's theory has two aspects that are reflections of the capitalist relations and the way they present themselves. First, the view that an effective 'character' is an attribute of the organisation of the ego, and that a well-organised ego guarantees a rational picture of reality. This is within individualism, because if the external world is socially structured it is structured irrationally; this comes out in Freudian theory only in the way it appears while living in that reality, that is that people feel that they are acting as individuals, and so failures are felt as personal failures, as being inadequate, ineffective personalities.

Secondly, the real impossibility of effectual action by individuals was reflected in Freud's deep social pessimism. Freud was not hopeful about social action and social change. But he put the cause of the intractability of society in the immutability of the human instincts, which continue to be active from within individuals' unconsciousnesses. In his theory, egos are very fragile affairs, and the kinds of impulses they restrain or partially restrain, mean that any social advance must rest on further repression. Greater altruism (which is what Freud thought would be the basis of socialism – again a change in individuals not social relations) could only be gained at the cost of more unconscious hostility, hence more guilt and neurosis. So social advance was a contradictory objective.

This is to place the limits on social change in a natural relation between instinctual man and society, not in the relations of any specific social formation. This is not an incidental consequence of his theory, but is founded on original, basic, assumptions and models of the individual as an instinctual biological entity, separate from, but relating to, the external world, physical, or now, social.

Reduction to sexuality

As we explained earlier, the different social relations of capitalism are dissociated. For example, the formation of intellectuality in the school is split off from the formation of sexuality, and from the formation of emotions, in the family. One of the effects of this is that they combine in a way that people are not able to be conscious of while living within them. Within the family, the different relations combine so that the dynamics of one, say sexuality, can come to result in another relation, say the domestic economic ones. An example would be the way the economic work of the woman in the home, which includes cooking for the man, comes to signify a sexual-emotional act towards him, so much that it actually is a sexual-emotional act. Freud theorises these effects of dissociation between social relations, but only at the level of effects, appearances. His theory starts from the family. Where capitalism concentrates sexuality in the private world of the family, so that sex and emotions are experienced as the basis of the other relations there, he actually theorises this in a way that makes all relations, in other spheres as well, as being determined by sexuality. He took the way sexuality and emotionality are experienced as the basis of other relations in the family, and made this a universal attribute of mental processes, instead of seeing it as an effect of the specific ways sexuality is put into relation with other things in capitalism.

As an example, let us look at the way intellectuality and sexuality seem to be related in the way we experience them, how Freud understands this, and how the theory reflects the reality.

Capitalism characteristically splits intellectuality and sexual relations. They are felt both as different and antagonistic areas of mental life, and are opposed to each other in popular ideology. For men, the split is most characteristic. For women it doesn't work so often; their thinking seems more often to get swamped by their feelings, so that the two get hopelessly entangled with each other. In fact one aspect of the split between thought and feeling at its most extreme, is the split between men as thinkers and women as feelers.

Freud's theory is that intellectuality and sexuality are split and antagonistic to each other because of the role of thought in repressing sexuality. Thought as such rests on sexual repression, as does consciousness, and different modes of thought represent the variations in the way repression was carried out and maintained. The other feature, the entanglements that occur between thought and feeling, are due either to thought being used as an ego defence against desire, in which case it substitutes itself for feeling; or as a result of inadequate repression, the unconscious desires oversexualise thought, and interfere with its own proper, rational, principles. In both cases sexuality is made to be the determining factor, explicable in terms of individual mental dynamics.

This is Freud's theory. But as we argued in the introduction, and later, the split between the family and the school; the sexual division of labour; the way that sexual and emotional formation happens away from intellectual formation so that thinking is something you learn to do about everything but your sexuality and feelings: all these are social relations which dissociate thought and feeling. Moreover, as we said about ourselves, when thought and feelings do form a basis of a relationship like a political-intellectual couple, their interaction is governed by the fact that they are combined in the personal relationship, the institution where sexual-emotional relations have a particular predominance, so that thinking easily becomes subordinate to the dynamics of the emotional sexual relations.

The particular way intellectual and sexual relations combine, which affects the way they interact, will depend on the institution in which they are. The way they interact at work, at school or university, will be different from the way they interact within the personal relationship. Again, because Freud took the family in abstraction, only from within the personal relationship, he saw only the effects of the infiltration of other relations and activities by the sexual dynamic. He then generalised this to all other institutions and activities of society. Though he did theorise sexuality and thought as being dissociated, his sexual reductionism makes it a universal property of the human mind, of the individual. This is especially obvious and crude in his theory of intellectual dullness, which he saw as resulting from repression of infantile sexual curiosity: this shows a failure to see the way that education in a class society suppresses any curiosity in the vast mass of the population.

Theory of sexuality

Givenness is a feature of sexual relations and feelings under capitalism. Freud reproduces it in his theory. The lived experience of givenness is that sexual relationships are formed because people have sexual feelings and emotions for each other. Families are formed from generation to generation on the same kinds of emotional patterns, and feelings are an objective part (not the only part) of the social mechanism by which the family is reproduced. These feelings feel just given: you just have feelings, they come upon you, they seem to be the more uncontrollable part of your personality with a force of their own, natural, not being experienced either as a social imposition or as social in origin. There is a corresponding ideology of feelings as irrational, and an ideal that they ought to have the quality of spontaneity and irresistability – love comes out of the blue and sexual attraction just happens. There is also a belief that feelings exist inside and you can discover 'what you really feel'. And that what you feel shouldn't be gainsaid by reason and calculation, which is cold and will damage you, if you don't express what you feel.

Freud undermines this ideology at one level, and explains the lived experience by giving a demystifying account of the sources of given feelings: feelings seem to come upon one irresistibly and irrationally from within because they are unconscious of their source. They are compulsive because the person feeling them isn't aware of their real content. Their 'real' meaning lies in the past, and by psychoanalysis, can be discovered to be still operating within the person. Adult sexual relationships are formed on the basis of feelings like this, given ones, because the Oedipus complex created in the child an unconscious structure of feelings, constantly pressing to be acted out, and so is the irresistible force, precisely because it is unconscious. Because the content of what was repressed is an emotional complex associated with sexual desire for parents, this emotional complex will be the basis of adult sexual relationships, the driving force behind any personal involvements with other people. The overwhelming power of attraction sex can have, and the compulsiveness of emotional infatuation, are due to this repression of instinctual sexual energy.

So Freud turns what in experience is a feeling of naturalness and givenness into a theory which makes givenness a property of emotionality and sexuality as such, arising from their instinctual basis and the infantile conflicts between sexual instincts and reality, leading inevitably to the creation of an unconscious in the individual. This deromanticises love and sexual attraction, and at this level it is a blow against the ideologies of love and sexual potency. But his theory still basically takes feelings as given, even reinforcing this by locating their qualities and origin in natural instinctual origins. Freud therefore takes as given, natural and general human qualities, what are in fact the effects of dissociation. As we argued dissociation entails that, due to the untheorised nature of the historical emergence of capitalist relations, each type of relation, sexual, economic, political, etc, has its own mode of operation, without any conscious articulation between them. As a result, emotions are given a force of their own, a trajectory of their own. But Freud takes this specifically capitalist form of emotionality and sexuality, as inherent and natural to emotions and sex themselves.

This leads to another example, comparing the reality and Freud's theory of it. In the existing social relations, sex, especially, is made to have a place that isn't connected with anything else except itself and certain kinds of feelings, so people only have their early sexual formation in childhood (and the way sex and feelings connect there), as a possible basis for their adult relations. It is particularly clear in the case of the traditional marriage: the way the different social relations fit together in their present is determining the structure of their feelings, by reproducing the structures which formed their feelings in the past: feelings are not just caused by structures inside the mind, imprinted from the past.

The woman in a relationship like this has a primarily emotional-sexual role, linked with caring, towards the husband. This is the same relation his mother had to him. The man has the role of going out to work, doing the active things in the outside world, making decisions, the same as the wife's father had, and all men ever since. The structure of social relations in the new adult family makes the husband invest his emotions in his wife as he did in his mother, and split this off from his other activities, because the two are split, not just as a consequence of a split in his head. And his wife will relate to him with the ambivalence of a child to the competent father because he is in a more commanding position than she. And if her resentment includes unacknowledged frustration at being deprived of the love of women, as Freud thinks, this is because the family does individualise women into units with a man, and does atomise women and antagonise them to one another, and so she is deprived of the love of women, not only in infantile phantasy.

Givenness, therefore, is a quality of sexuality that comes from the existing capitalist reality of sexual relations, within which adults find themselves and have to be sexual. It is not a quality that comes from the nature of individual people, rooted in a past which formed them — a phantasy only in the mind. That past external world which formed individuals was itself structured, and was not just a physical milieu for a biological entity.

One important aspect of both past and present structures which Freud theorises, but only at the level of effects, is the way sexism enters the family. The evaluation of the penis over the female sexual organs, by both boy and girl children, is a fundamental plank of Freud's theory of sexual development and also the development of the superego, and hence culture. Freud writes of the superiority of the penis as a self-evident fact, in comparison with the clitoris. This is also true of the child's fear of the father, an integral part of the Oedipal theory: the child's fear of punishment by the father, and not the mother, is what leads to repression and identification. Now, both these conditions for the Oedipus complex and its resolution (the valuation of the penis, and the fear), derive from the objective power of the father in the family, which is not the object of Freud's work. But it isn't enough to say, as many of his apologists do, 'that wasn't what he was concerned with, he was only concerned with the level of what actually goes on within the family, and wasn't looking at what the social context was'.

This isn't enough, because taking the social relations of sexism for granted makes his theory of what happens within the family into an ideological reflection of sexism. The clitoris is devalued to the extent that his theory makes it biologically necessary to eliminate it altogether as a source of sexual activity. If, as Freud did, you only look at the inter-actions in the family between the small child and each of its parents, then it seems inevitable that the penis must be valued higher than the clitoris, because the family itself seems natural and given. But it is the separation of production from consumption, which places the woman in the home and the man out in the world, that is the basis for the child's and Freud's equation of the male with activity and sexuality, and the woman with passivity and receptivity, and this leads to the overvaluation of the penis and the denial of the clitoris.

Freud has theorised the perceptions of a child in the family, without moving beyond the child's own framework, the interactions between the individual child and the parents, as individuals, within the family. This is to reflect the capitalist reality of sexism in a very basic way. The given perceptions of the penis are left at face value in his theory. Where there is a sexist consciousness, Freud not only makes chauvinist statements himself, but his theory makes male domination necessary for civilisation itself. 'Penis envy', 'castration complex', aren't just dispensable bits of Freud's theory: without them there would be no repression and no culture. By making the theory of sexual development rest on the Oedipus complex, castration complex, and the primacy of the penis, he converts male domination into the universal motor of natural human development, not just the specific consciousness of a phallocratic culture. This is just one example of why it is illegitimate to accept Freud's theory of mental processes, while rejecting some unpalatable aspects of the content, like his theory of women.

Emotional individualism is a lived experience and a social relation of capitalist reality, and Freud's theory makes emotions and sexual feelings the attributes of individuals.

Part of what is felt about feelings as they are lived is the sense that they originate, have their ultimate source, within yourself. It is almost a definition of feelings that they come from inside individuals, just because they are felt by individuals. It would be almost nonsensical to say feelings could have any other source in capitalist common sense. This is also true of other individualisms, e.g. feeling that you are the individual origin of your own thoughts, actions.

Correspondingly, love and sexual feelings are felt for other people for their individual qualities, for themselves as individuals. Romantic ideology of love pictures two individuals in love as uniquely fitted to each

132

other. People's individualism is involved in sexual relations in more ways than just sexual: in existing sexual relations, people's identity is affirmed or threatened by the relationship.

Freud deals a severe blow to the romantic idea and lived experience that love and sexual desires are for each other's special lovelinesses, by his theory that these feelings are based on the phantasies of the lover, not the qualities of the loved one. He also gives a more theoretical basis to the sense that the way one lives is an inherent part of one's own personality, by, for example, his notions of anaclitic and narcissistic love, which traces differences in the way identity is affirmed in love to childhood object-choices in relation to the person's own ego. But he reproduces the individualism of lived experience by placing the source of the feelings inside each individual instead of the social system that individualises people.

Freud undermines the capitalist common sense, that individuals are the sources of their own actions and thoughts, by taking causation and effective action away from the conscious thinking subject, the 'I' which feels and thinks, plans, intends things. His theory only gives limited effectiveness to the aims of the ego. He says, no, things are not as they appear, there are sources of our feelings and thoughts that we are not aware of, and which therefore control us. But he locates this hidden source of action and feeling inside the individual still, the individual unconscious, and the result of this is to eliminate all social relations: there are only individuals with laws of operation within them, not between them. There are no social laws at all, not even of the couple as a social relation. What appears to be a sexual relation between two people, in Freud's theory, is not really a relationship at all.

Now this theoretical conclusion reflects in an extreme form the way that capitalism, by its structure of social relations, produces individualism as a social relation. So emotional individualism, which is an attribute of a specific social sexual system, becomes in Freud's hands, a natural attribute of people. This is the same kind of relation to capitalist reality that we see in his theory of sex. Kinds of sexual feelings are the effect of specific sexual relations. Freud theorises the feelings characteristic of dissociated capitalist sexual relations as natural and immutable attributes of individual people conceived as biological organisms.

We can see this very clearly, as a last example, from the way Freud tried to say what sex in general, as a human function, was for: was it for pleasure, for reproduction, he asks? Did it have to be repressed in the interests of biological reproduction? the reproduction of society? These normative ideas about sex are about sex as such, not sex as a sexual social relation. His questions are, we can now see, the wrong questions to be asking (and led to the absurdity of theories like the need for women to 'change' from clitoral to vaginal sexuality). Think of the way sexuality has changed in its relation to reproduction since Freud was working. This has happened as the religious and monogamous forms of sexual relations have eased, and has been aided by the technology of contraception, as well as such profoundly economic and social changes as the need of the economy for women workers.

Freud's view of the necessity for women to develop a whole range of feminine and sexual character traits is really a necessity limited to a particular set of social relations in which he found himself, and this goes for his whole theory of the differentiation between the sexes and homosexuality. Because he had an ahistorical, asocial theory, he had an ahistorical conception of what sex is, sex in the abstract; and therefore he had a semi-biological and instinctual theory of masculinity and femininity. This made the distinction based on very specific cultural pictures of how women are (modest, passive, vain, not inventive, morally weak, envious, dependent of character, selfish and of weak social and community interest, less capacity for sublimating instincts, for thought, more prone to neurosis, less prone to further development of mind and character after the age of thirty, highly inclined to sexual frigidity – all this and more in 'Femininity', New Introductory Lectures), into a theory of how women should develop according to universal biological and social imperatives.

Some strands of sexual politics, close to Reich, simply urge people to express sex more fully, sexual feelings which are locked up within the individual. Society is conceived of just in terms of prohibitions and restrictions. But to abstract sex like this is an extension of the way it is already abstracted, and so, in the same manner as Freud's theory, reinforces the way we are unconsciously tied to the social relations of capitalism. Sex is not a biological given, simply, which only has to be released from inside people. Sexual changes need changes in the specific social relations of sexuality, and their replacement by other, equally general social relations.

PSYCHOANALYSIS IS A BOURGEOIS AND SEXIST THEORY AND PRACTICE

In the first section on Freud, psychoanalysis was put in the general context of the capitalist division of labour; the division between theorisers and theorised about; and of the capitalist split between theory and lived experience. But just as the division between theorisers and theorised about creates a specific social relation between them, so also there is a specific social relation between theory and lived experience, not just absence of any relation. So, in the previous section, we showed that there were multiple correspondences, if indirect ones, between psychoanalytical theory, ideological everyday consciousness, and the structure of capitalist sexual relations. Now in this section, we shall try to show how these correspondences are created, in what specific ways the particular theoretical concepts are practically related to capitalist sexual relations.

Another way of putting it is that we want to show how the theoretical knowledge, which a capitalist expert knower has, comes to exist at all — rather than everyone just going on with only the lived, untheoretical, experience of capitalist sexual relations. For it seems important to understand how the division between theory and lived experience is created.

We have argued that lived sexual relations under capitalism are not themselves theorised by those that live them, and that consciousness of them is not theoretical, because they emerged in the way that all capitalist social relations have, without any conscious political and social construction by the majority of people. We live the effects of historical changes which we did not consciously bring about. Historically, for a long time, capitalism had no theory of sexuality at all: moralities, certainly, but not theories. Freud represents the emergence of a theory of sexuality. It emerged on the basis of the psychoanalytical situation, in which, as we explained in the first section, mental treatment by hypnosis was creating a new way that capitalism had of regulating its disorders, by defining them as mental or psychological disorders, as opposed to physical or moral ones.

The first point to make therefore, is that the psychoanalytical situation, and within it the relation between the therapist and the patient, is a distinctive one, different from the reality of lived sexual relations. It is this psychoanalytical situation that is theorised, and not, at least not directly, the sexual relations as they are lived. So the question of how theory relates to the lived experience of sexual relations, is more fundamentally a question of how the psychoanalytical situation differs from, but relates to, the situation of just living the existing structures of capitalist sexual relations. It is important that the psychoanalytical situation is a therapeutic situation, in which capitalism is regulating its disorders. The theory is based on a therapy, a cure, a disorder, and only then is it extrapolated to be a theory of the order, of the normality. The significance of this is that, just as the economic disorders of capitalism have their own respective techniques of regulation (e.g. creating mass unemployment), which do nothing to change the economic relations that entail those particular disorders, so the psychoanalytical situation also has a parasitic relation to the existing sexual relations: its practice does not create a totally new social form of sexual relations, but creates a special regulatory situation alongside the existing one, and theorises about that.

It is because the psychoanalytical situation is 'outside' the normal, untheorised practice of lived sexual relations, that the theory is possible at all: through thinking about the effects of the systematic actions of the theorist (the method), a systematic theory becomes possible. But the limitation is, in Freud's case, that these systematic actions are outside the normal relations. They are not a systematic theorised practice to change the existing relations, or to construct a new social reality.

The psychoanalytic situation

Here we shall just look at the structure of the psychoanalytical situation before looking at the effects that it produces on people.

What is special about the psychoanalytical practice that transforms the reality of lived sexual relations to make theory possible? (We are basing the following account largely on a reading of Freud's papers on technique, and on the numerous accounts he gives of his methods as they changed, as well as on some personal experience.) There are a number of ways in which the psychoanalytical situation transforms the structure of normal lived social relations. To set the scene: the patient normally lies on a couch behind which, and out of his sight, sits the analyst. This breaks the normal face to face dialogue, since only the analyst can see the expressions of the patient's face, not vice versa. The 'first rule' of psychoanalysis breaks even further with normal communication. One person is to speak without reserve all the thoughts that come into his head, so altering the normal gap between thinking and speaking which is essential to dialogue, and making the speech of the patient a kind of compulsorily spoken-out monologue. More important perhaps even than this, is that it is not usual for the communication between two individuals to be structured in such a way that one person initiates all the statements, and reveals all his thoughts, while the other person does not reply by making statements on his own account, but instead just makes comments about the other's. These characteristics of the psychoanalytical situation transform the structure of communication, and create a very special form of social relation of communication between two people.

But apart from these changes in the structure of communication, the psychoanalytical situation does two further and interconnected things. First, it abstracts the individual. And secondly, in so doing, it breaks all the links between talking/thinking and living/doing. The 'conversation' takes place outside all day-to-day relations that a person has. The therapist only relates to the patient as the patient's thoughts about himself or about the world 'outside'. You could say that the situation abstracts the mental. As a result, the therapist can only deal with 'thoughts about' things, as if they were only thoughts. So his problem becomes one of whether thoughts are more or less valid, more or less phantasising — problems are placed in the head, not in reality. Again this psychoanalytical situation is quite different from one in which talking and thinking are inserted in ongoing relationships, ongoing activities.

These are the principal changes, which set the framework of everything that goes on within the psychoanalytic situation. As such they are the continuous background to the special effects created by it, which we shall go into soon. The important point is that this situation is a social situation, a particular form of relationship different from but alongside, the existing social relationships in which both therapist and patient live. As such it does transform the reality of existing social relationships, if in a minimal way. This will enable us to understand more what the relationship is between capitalist lived experience of existing social relations, and a distinct but parallel basis for theorising them. For, the minimal transformations brought about by the psychoanalytical situation, act upon what is brought in from outside. The patient brings his everyday consciousness into the situation, as it has been produced within his existing relationships, the family, sexual and work relationships. Because the psychoanalytical situation is a limited special form of social relation alongside the rest of reality, its transformations are only transformations of what is brought in from outside. In this way, the reality which the theorist theorises inside the psychoanalytical situation is integrally related to the consciousness of existing capitalist relations produced outside it. Both the inside and the outside are conditions of the reality theorised inside.

The effects of the psychoanalytic situation

We shall now try to look at the links between the effects created by the psychoanalytical situation and the concepts of the psychoanalytical theory outlined previously, so to account for the complex relation between ideological theory and ideological consciousness. This can't be done simply by relating given concepts — say, the unconscious — to one particular aspect of the practice of psychoanalysis and its effects. Rather, different aspects coincide to sustain a relation between the conceptual structure as a whole and the different effects created by the practice. In looking at the relation between the theory of the unconscious and the practice of psychoanalysis, for example, it's impossible to deal with the aspect of unconsciousness apart from the aspect of individualism. There is an abstraction of the mental, but at the same time abstraction of the individual in the psychoanalysed situation. It is the way the different aspects of the social relation between therapist and patient coincide that makes up the 'special reality' being theorised.

And in saying they coincide, we mean that Freud himself did not theorise his practice sufficiently to consciously articulate the different aspects of what he was doing to the patient. This brings up the general point which is also present in the relation between Freud's theory and practice: he himself did not theorise the psychoanalytical situation as a special form of social relation, a transformation of social relations, with special effects inherent in them as social relations. Instead, he himself simply looks at the patient as the object of his theory, and takes the thoughts emanating from the individual patient as expressions of the individual, not as effects of the social relation. He regards himself as having a passive relation of an external observer to the patient. In a certain sense, within the context, he is. But not in creating the context, not in bringing about the three major structural changes indicated above, which bring about a specific social relation between theorist and theorised.

To begin with, we'll arbitrarily start at one point in his theory, his concept of the unconscious, and gradually unfold its ramifications, in relation to the coincident different aspects of his practice. In the first section, hypnosis was seen to be an instrument by which the particular psychological theory of the unconscious was developed. With the advent of psychoanalysis proper, hypnosis was dropped. The theory of the unconscious continued, but it too was changed: changes in theory went along with changes in practice, changes in the reality being theorised. Freud had seen hypnosis not only as a means which gave special access to thoughts and memories not available to the patient's waking consciousness. He also saw it as a power the therapist had over the patient. Under hypnosis, the therapist could suggest things to the patient, even give direct commands to get better, with effects that were not possible when the patient was in normal consciousness. Freud, rejecting a number of semi-mystical explanations of hypnosis, considered his power to be akin to the power of suggestion that a father or mother has over their children; or the kind of mutual suggestibility of people in love. He then considered this kind of power as a positive thing, a kind of psychological power necessary to bring about psychological changes in the patient.

Freud abandoned hypnosis for two main reasons: he couldn't hypnotise all patients, or at least often not to sufficient depth; and he found that, just because of the emotional relationship going with the extreme suggestibility of the patient, akin to being in love with the therapist, hypnosis seemed to induce emotional dependence on the therapist which proved counterproductive. The cure lasted only for so long as the treatment, and ended with the end of the emotional relationship to the therapist.

He abandoned his powers of suggestion over the patient, therefore. But at the same time, he abandoned what had been a specially direct access to the unconscious thoughts of the patient. Freud, however, still 'knew' the unconscious was there. So if he wasn't able to get at it directly when the patient was in normal consciousness, that meant that there was resistance to becoming conscious of those unconscious ideas. He only 'discovered' the dynamics of resistance when he abandoned his powers of bypassing it through hypnosis. But was the resistance in the patient, or was it an effect of the changed social relation between the therapist and the patient? Freud, in a typical mystification of his own practice took the former view. He considered that he had discovered a new mental dynamic, entirely internal to the patient, a force of repression which made ideas resistant to becoming conscious. We don't need to deny that people are unconscious of things. But it's one thing to say that people are unconscious and that there are social blocks to becoming conscious while living within social relations of capitalism which were formed unconsciously. It's another to say that that unconsciousness is a property of an individual mind and that the blocks are entirely internal to it. In the first case, it would be intelligible that there would be resistances to becoming conscious – which are not abstractly mental – but as part of the resistances to social practices of changing social relations.

Yet psychoanalysis is itself a social practice – which for example abstracts the individual from his normal lived relations – and it depends on this social practice for the patient to 'become conscious' in the particular way he does in that situation – he would not do it spontaneously. So the resistance is relative to a social practice. Changes in Freud's powers meant that what was open to him before was no longer. The point is that making people conscious is in any event a social practice: the psychoanalytical or pre-psychoanalytical situations are just special instances of this. The resistances to his practice are directly linked to limitations of his practice — the fact that the abstraction of the individual and the abstraction of the mental made it impossible for his practice to change the social relations outside the psychoanalytical situation. Nonetheless Freud, as if his method wasn't a social practice at all, but an external eye into the internal workings of the mind, ascribes everything to the inherent properties of the individual mind. We'll see this coming up again and again: what is a property of the social interaction between therapist and patient is attributed to the patient's own internal mental processes.

This self-mystification goes along with his understanding that he had abandoned all his powers over the patient when he abandoned hypnosis, so that within the psychoanalytical situation, he regarded himself as playing a purely passive role. This combined with another crucial switch in his theory, additional to the theory of resistance. For whereas before he had seen hypnosis as making the patient fall in love with the doctor, he now saw himself as doing nothing. Patients still kept on falling in love with him, or having emotional reactions to him. But he now saw this as nothing to with what he, as therapist who revealed nothing and just sat listening, was making happen. It was something the patients were laying on him. And because, in his logic, there was nothing in the actual situation to bring about emotional relations to him — no real basis for love or hostile reactions — after all, the therapist was the external observer — these emotional reactions had to come out of the unconscious ideas that the patient had about the doctor. They could not be realistic emotional reactions, because the therapist did not present his person at all. So it was only to images the patient had in the head that the patient was reacting, mostly images of parents, mother or more often father. In other words, the patient was transferring onto the therapist his emotional reactions to unconscious images of other people. Whereas in the normal lived relations outside, emotional individualism or falling in love appears 'natural' and related to the person loved, and this is sustained by popular ideology and consciousness, the emotional relation to the therapist is seen as a fantasy, having nothing to do with the therapist as a person. This then is used as the basis of a theory of love in general.

But in looking at things like this, Freud was replacing the popular and romantic ideology of love with a theory which was even more abstract emotional and individualist. He did so because he failed to see how the social relation in the psychoanalytical situation created modifications of the social relations outside. It was only because he could think that he was doing nothing that he could think that the emotional reactions were simply projected or transferred onto him, and only because he thought that he was theorising the patient not his social relation to him, and that there wasn't any social relation, that the emotional reactions were to ideas in the head.

What we have to consider is what the relation is between the psychoanalytical situation with its effects, and the reality of lived relations outside. For while that reality exists outside, it is obvious that there are going to be expressions of some of the same kinds of emotions (created outside) inside. But there are also ways in which the psychoanalytical situation itself reproduces, and in so doing exaggerates, aspects of social relations that exist outside. It does seem amazing that Freud could think of himself as an external observer who did not induce transference. The fact that one person is giving all the understanding and the other person is doing all the self-revealing; the fact that being asked to speak every intimate thought that comes into your head is not itself without significance; these facts amount to a special social relationship between two people. Many of the aspects correspond, if in exaggerated form, with the structural aspects of children's relations to parents. After all, to reveal all the intimacies to someone who keeps his own sexual life completely obscure is the kind of relationship which is most likely to reproduce the ways in which people as children have related to parents who disclose nothing to children.

Further aspects are likely to induce a particularly abstract form of emotional attachment, precisely because of the way in which self-revelation is taken out of normal everyday practical relations: the relationship is decontextualised. As an intuitive example, not so exaggerated as the psychoanalytical situation, one can think of those 'falling in love' experiences which occur in similarly out of 'normal context' situations, the most renowned being the holiday affair. At the same time, this decontextualisation is taking the individual out of the context of normal social reproduction of sexual relations, and restricting the relation between the therapist and the patient to an exchange of thoughts. It is therefore viewed by Freud as an entirely individual act of the patient, a mental fantasy, emanating from the patient's internal mental dynamics. It is not seen as a transformed version of the normal social forms of emotionality corresponding to specific social relations.

So, once again, Freud reinforces in a new form, the individualism which is evident in the consciousness of lived relations outside the psychoanalytical situation. He does not theorise that situation as a particular variant of social relations that exist outside, or as a social relation at all. He does not theorise transference love as an effect of the decontextualisation of the social relation between patient and therapist, or other aspects of the social relation. Instead he attributes the effects of this social relation entirely into the patient's head, and uses it as the basis of the theory of mental dynamics which underly the Oedipus complex.

Transference love is one of the principle special effects produced by the psychoanalitical social relation. Now, for Freud, the cure is effected through the working out of these unrealistic, fantasy relations the patient has to the therapist. This means that repressed unconscious ideas are expressed, and during the course of being expressed, can gradually be made conscious. In this, the role of the therapist is not to emotionally react himself, or to reveal himself. Instead, the therapist interprets the patient. This leads directly to another way in which Freud ascribes to the internal dynamics of the patient what is an intrinsic part of the social relation between therapist and patient: the division between ego and unconscious. For, in the complete division of roles between therapist and patient, a specific relation is set up between one person doing all the emoting and the other doing all the understanding. We've seen how the psychoanalytical situation abstracts the patient's thoughts about things from any connection to lived relations outside, including within the psychoanalytical situation itself, where the therapist does not enter into a relation with the patient as part of his everyday life. So, when the patient does all the emoting, it can only be in the head, a fantasy emotional relation, not a realisable one. Because the emotion is based on an unconscious idea, the therapist's role is to reveal the fantasy for what it is. Everything is made into a mental event: there are the patient's unconscious emotional reactions to thoughts about the therapist, and then the therapist's interpretation of them.

What the analyst does then is essentially to re-interpret the patient's consciousness of his emotional reactions. By doing this, the analyst hopes to re-direct emotional currents, with the patient properly understanding them for what they are. The psychoanalyst only re-interprets the (patient's consciousness of) the world; the point is not to change it. This is because, ignoring that the social practice of analysis creates a specific social relation with its own effects, Freud looks at what the patient does as only being a false consciousness: no question of a reality to change.

So, the social relation between the therapist and the patient is between one person who acts as a supposedly external source of observations and interpretations about what is a realistic thought and what is fantasy; and the other person supposedly emotes to unconscious ideas he has in his head about the therapist. This division of roles (connected to the whole division between theorist and theorised talked of in the first section), which is the basis of the whole definition of what is reality and fantasy since Freud deems there to be no basis for it in the real relation between patient and therapist, is then attributed to the internal mental dynamics of the patient. There is the ego, searching to give correct interpretations of reality; and there is the unconscious as the origin of fantasy. The opposition between thought, as the reality principle, and irrational unconscious feelings is built into the social relation of the psychoanalytical situation. But Freud sees it as a universal property of the human mind. That it is 'all in the mind' is also a social aspect of the social relation; but 'being all in the mind' is also made by Freud into a property of the mind as such.

The instincts

The role of the analyst, as understood by Freud, is to 'strengthen the ego', i.e. to be able to tell what is fantasy and what is reality in the patient's consciousness, and to give a helping hand to reality. This restriction of the analyst's role merely to re-interpreting the patient's consciousness, means that the analyst can change very little, can do very little, but re-interpret. Once more this weakness of the analyst's powers to transform, are ascribed to the internal mental dynamics of the patient. The ego only interprets, and guides forces within the patient that are basically outside the patient's control. These forces are above all the instincts. The ego can only lead the instincts to their aim, whereas the instincts themselves are immutable. All that can change is the degree to which the ego can make sure that the instincts make realistic and effective contacts with the outside world.

While there is no doubt that Freud simply 'imported' the concepts of instinct from biology, there being no proper and independent foundation for a theory of instincts within the psychoanalytical situation, nonetheless, because of the limitation of the powers of the therapist to those of interpretation, the psychoanalytical situation could not contradict biological concepts of innate forces, and in Freud, these were re-inforced: the psychological individualism, coupled with the concepts of the individual unconscious mind, could complement the idea of a biological individual with given innate properties.

But nonetheless, although we can't go into it here, Freud's theory of the instincts did change in the course of his lifetime, often as a consequence of his analysis of the relation between the ego and unconscious fantasy we have just discussed. One of the clearest and most illuminating examples of the way he used psychoanalytical evidence to support a speculative biological idea of instinct, was his invention of the death instinct. For, the idea of a death instinct is closely related to the 'discovery' of forces within the patient which made him resistant to being cured. This is particularly clear in two papers in which Freud asks himself whether a cure is ever complete, or will last whatever happens to the patient. He thinks that because there is no such guarantee, and because even while being analysed, the patient resists being cured, this is evidence of the existence of a death instinct, a basic unwillingness to live. This is only an illustration which highlights the general relation between the analyst, as representative of the ego, against emotions, or instincts. Because of the limitations of his own practice, his own powers to change things, through re-interpretation, he ascribes given properties to the object which are unchangeable by nature. If you can't change a property of the object you theorise it as an unchangeable property.

In this respect, Freud reproduces in the psychoanalytical situation a variant of what exists outside. The capitalist relation between consciousness and the untheorised practice of social relations, is that consciousness does ride along passively interpreting a reality that seems unchangeable, a reality that certainly can't be changed simply by re-interpretation. In the psychoanalysis, where this relation is individualised, this relation between consciousness and its material practical base under capitalism, is converted into a universal ahistorical relation between the ego and the instincts.

Psychoanalysis is a bourgeois and sexist theory and practice

The question now is how all these effects of psychoanalytical practice and its limits link in together, and why therefore Freud has a mystified understanding of his own relation to his patients, causing him to attribute aspects of the social relation between the therapist and patient to the internal dynamics of the individual human mind. The main point is that the limitations of psychoanalytical practice are social limitations. consequent upon the elitist nature of the relation between therapist and patient. To change sexuality and to construct sexual relations on a general social level, requires a mass practice, where interpreting and changing reality go hand in hand. Freudian theory is based on a practical social relation which eliminates the possibility of such a relation between theory and mass practice. The abstraction of the individual expresses only the fact that in the elitist division of labour, the experts can, if they are to remain the experts, only act to make small corrective measures on individuals (or at most small groups). Similarly this abstraction of the individual itself means that the actions the expert can take are limited. In the case of psychoanalysis, this limitation takes the form of the therapist only being able to interpret things, where interpretation is cut off from changing things. Experts can't change society, they can only regulate the disorders of society in a minimal way, by trying to change those individuals designated deviant from the existing normality: the pathology is directly related to a theory of what is normality.

The fact that the theory is based on a limited transformation of existing capitalist reality, in a way which both accentuates the individualism of the emotions and their abstractness, is crucial in determining the relation between the theory and the lived consciousness of capitalist relations. For, the effects brought about by the practice, and its limitations, are theorised as the natural properties of the human mind, because, for Freud's elitist practice, there was no other reality he could theorise. It is because the limits are real limits, not just in the head; limits on the practical basis of a knowledge based on an elitist division of labour; that in relation to that practice, reality really is unchangeable. The elitist theorist is locked within it. It is the only reality he can know. For him it is the universal reality, none beyond it.

So, there is a theory of immutable natural instincts in relation to which conscious thought is only a passive adjunct. This is a direct consequence of its relation to a practice which is not a mass, social and conscious practice to change social reality by social means. That is why any theory which rests similarly on the idea of there being some basic biological sexual urge, against which society acts repressively, repeats the Freudian ideology at its most insidious.

This is particularly true of Reich. The theory of an immutable source of biological energy, instinctual sex, is in its origin an idea which attributes to people some immutable properties which transcend history. The demand for a more spontaneous expression of this instinctual energy as against social repression, is only placing at a different level than Freud's, a profoundly anti-political conception of man, instead of one in which sexual relations are specific historical social-sexual relations, with their specific contradictions, and in which the political problem is to construct new social forms of sexual relations. As with the concept of instinct in its origins in Freud, the Reichian concepts of biological instinct versus social repression is one which makes it impossible to think about what concrete social forces, at which particular times in history, are going to develop a political practice of sexuality that amounts to something more than a 'permissiveness liberation' which capitalism has already got well in hand: mobilising a biological instinct present at all times in all people, actively denies the reality of sexism, in which women in particular do have a different relation to the particular capitalist sexual relations. The problem is that a demand for expression of 'natural' sexual energy does have totally different significance for women than for men in the present historical sexual relations. As such it is only a variant of the Freudian sexism which makes specific sexist relations of capitalism discussed earlier, into normal, natural and universal ones. The demand for greater spontaneity comes from a much more basic, and anti-political assumption of a universal human nature.

The basis for this critique of Freud, and of some of the radical variants of Freud, is that Freudianism is not only a theory, but a generalised social practice; its concepts bear a practical relation to our everyday consciousness of existing sexual relations. We have tried to show how Freudian theory does present a variant of many implicit assumptions held in common sense, and spells them out theoretically. It is possible to reject the theory without making that a self-criticism of our own implicit assumptions about the individualism of feelings, about spontaneity and 'natural' sex; about givenness of our own feelings, etc. But these assumptions spelt out in theory might look like Freudian theory.

It's also possible to accept Freudian theory in a completely academic way, without seeing the way it does reinforce the assumptions which sustain existing personal relations under capitalism. It is because of the 'parasitic' practical relation between the reality of the psychoanalytical situation as a basis for theory, and existing sexual relations, that there is this relation between Freudian theory and everyday implicit assumptions. It's also because of this practical relation that there is a split between theory and experience, which makes possible either of these two false reactions to Freud: it's impossible that such a theory based on such a practice could ever be part of a mass practice to change untheorised lived relations. This is why we need to think of developing a theory, not in relation to some mini-situation alongside existing social reality, but to a practice of constructing a general social form of sexual relations, articulated with the other relations of the social formation.

Only in this way, by changing reality through a theorised practice on the basis of the specific historical contradictions within capitalist reality, will the relation between theory and lived consciousness, at present split, also be changed in society as a whole.